A Cultural History
of the
United States

■

Through the Decades

The 1900s

Adam Woog

Lucent Books, Inc., San Diego, California

Library of Congress Cataloging-in-Publication Data

Woog, Adam, 1953–
    The 1900s / by Adam Woog.
        p.   cm.—(A cultural history of the United States through
    the decades)
        Includes bibliographical references and index.
        Summary: Discusses the political, economic, and cultural life of
    the United States in the first decade of the twentieth century,
    including daily life, labor relations, the conservation movement,
    and transportation.
        ISBN 1-56006-550-8 (lib: alk. paper)
        1. United States—History—1901–1909—Juvenile literature.
    2. United States—Social life and customs—1865–1918—Juvenile
    literature. 3. Nineteen hundreds (Decade)—Juvenile literature.
    [1. United States—History—1901–1909. 2. United States—Social
    life and customs—1865–1918. 3. Nineteen hundreds (Decade)]
    I. Title. II. Series.
    E756.W94   1999
        973.91'1—dc21   98-27964
                                                                          CIP
                                                                           AC

Copyright 1999 by Lucent Books, Inc.
P.O. Box 289011, San Diego, California 92198-9011

Printed in the U.S.A.

Contents

Introduction

A crowded street in New York City in 1904 reveals the fashions and travel available to people at the turn of the century, an optimistic time for most Americans.

A Century Begins

As the twentieth century began, many Americans felt highly optimistic. The country seemed to be on the verge of a new era of peace, prosperity, and progress.

For one thing, the economy was booming. In the years since the Civil War, America had changed from a primarily agricultural to a mostly industrial nation. Manufacturing was now the main force driving the American economic engine, and the country was rivaling the top European nations in world trade, thanks to a wealth of raw materials, a ready workforce, and a knack for the practical application of technology.

There were other reasons to be optimistic. The national treasury had a substantial surplus. The recently fought Spanish-American War had been a spectacular victory, and America had emerged from it as a major voice in world affairs. Furthermore, technological innovations were making daily life easier and more pleasurable than ever before. In its lead editorial for January 1, 1900, the *New York Times* exclaimed,

> The year 1899 was a year of wonders. . . . It would be easy to speak of the twelve months just passed as the banner year were we not already confident that the distinction of highest records must presently pass to the year 1900. . . . The outlook on the threshold of the new year is extremely bright.[1]

Good Old Days?

This optimistic outlook has helped foster a belief among some observers today that the 1900s were "the good old days." They argue that at the turn of the century people were happier, politicians were more honest, and life was simpler and safer.

It is true that customs were generally simpler and more conservative. People usually married in their early twenties, for instance, and divorce was a scandalous state of affairs.

Attitudes about the sexes were also more formal. Men tipped their hats to ladies. A woman was chaperoned when in a room with a man not her husband. Most married women did not work outside the home, although many, even in relatively prosperous families, grew extra vegetables or took in laundry to supplement the household income. Altogether, only about 20 percent of all American women were employed outside the home.

Some aspects of life may have been simpler during the 1900s, but in some ways life was also more difficult and complicated. Historians Oscar Theodore Barck Jr. and Nelson Manfred Blake note, "For many Americans [the 1900s] were years of peace and promise, but for others they were years of tension when old institutions fell under criticism and the need for change was strongly felt."[2]

Problems

There were, indeed, many problems. Millions out of the nation's 76 million inhabitants lived in impoverished slums. Laws to protect workers against injury, or to protect consumers against diseased or dangerous food, were virtually nonexistent. Thousands of laborers, including children, toiled in dangerous and ill-paid jobs. Disease took thousands of lives and crippled thousands more. Medicines that people now take for granted, such as antibiotics and insulin, did not yet exist.

Angry voices were raised across the country demanding rights for women, minorities, and workers. Corruption among government officials

Wash day in New York City around the turn of the century shows how most people in these crowded tenements dried their laundry—with solar power.

was widespread. Furthermore, a small number of businessmen controlled a large proportion of the nation's wealth, and they often recklessly exploited the country's natural resources.

Nonetheless, even if "the good old days" were not always good, the overall mood as America began the new century was optimistic. The mood gave rise to several nicknames for the 1900s, including the Age of Optimism, the Age of Confidence, and the Age of Innocence.

Americans of the era, generally speaking, did not merely hope for the best: they expected it. They felt as though their country was special, and that they belonged to a remarkable people. A German writer, Emil Reich, noted at the time, "Americans are filled with such an implicit and absolute confidence in their Union and in their future success that any remark other than laudatory [flattering] is unacceptable to the majority of them." [3]

"That Damned Cowboy"

In 1900, using the jaunty campaign slogan "Four Years More of the Full Dinner Pail," President William McKinley was elected for a second term. In March 1901, he was sworn in. McKinley, a Republican, had been well liked during his first term, and it looked as though he would continue to be a popular leader for the new century.

Then everything changed.

In September 1901, McKinley attended the Pan-American Exposition in Buffalo, New York. As he stood in a reception line shaking hands, the presi- dent was approached by Leon Czolgosz, a twenty-eight-year-old Polish-American with a history of mental instability. Czolgosz shot McKinley with a pistol concealed in a handkerchief.

The president was rushed to a hospital by Secret Service agents. For a few days, it looked as though he would survive. His vice president, Theodore Roosevelt, confident that everything would be all right, went hiking in New York's Adirondack Mountains.

However, while returning down the mountainside, Roosevelt was notified by a messenger that McKinley had taken a

Leon Czolgosz shoots President McKinley at close range with a pistol that he had concealed in a handkerchief. His death propelled Theodore Roosevelt into the presidency.

Theodore Roosevelt

Theodore Roosevelt, the most important single person in America in the 1900s, was an enormous influence on action and thought both at home and abroad. According to writer Frederick Lewis Allen in *The Big Change*, "He struck a new keynote for the times, and it resounded all over America."

Roosevelt's endless energy, which one wit said made him like "a steam engine in trousers," made him an easy target for both parody and adoration. Most Americans delighted in his unique characteristics, and newspaper cartoonists loved to lampoon them: his flashing eyeglasses, huge grin, high-pitched voice and relentless, wide-ranging intellectual interest.

Teddy Roosevelt was born in New York City on October 27, 1858, to a well-to-do family. He led a privileged childhood, but was a sickly boy who suffered from weak eyesight and asthma. Determined to overcome his frailty, he became devoted to maintaining "the strenuous life" through constant exercise.

He also became a ferocious learner, reading as many as three books a day. While attending Harvard University, TR, as he was often known, began writing the first of his own twenty-four books. His breadth of knowledge spanned subjects as diverse as mammals, birds, military affairs, and art history.

At twenty-four, Roosevelt entered politics, an unusual move at the time for a young man of the upper class. He served in the New York State Assembly from 1881 to 1884. He also spent two years running a ranch in the Dakota Territory, ran unsuccessfully for mayor of New

Pictured is Theodore Roosevelt in his "Rough Rider" uniform.

York, and was appointed president of that city's Police Board.

President William McKinley made Roosevelt his assistant secretary of the navy, but when the United States declared war on Spain in 1898, a desk job proved too tame. Roosevelt formed a volunteer cavalry regiment, the Rough Riders, and led them in a famous charge up Cuba's San Juan Hill. Roosevelt became a national hero, a role he gladly accepted, and soon after ran successfully for governor of New York.

Roosevelt became a prominent spokesman for progressive reforms, and in 1900 he ascended to national politics, becoming McKinley's vice presidential nominee as the president campaigned for a second term.

turn for the worse. A later messenger informed him that McKinley was dead.

Roosevelt, the young and charismatic former governor of New York, hurriedly returned to Washington and was sworn in as McKinley's successor. At forty-two, Teddy Roosevelt was at that point the youngest person to have ever reached the nation's highest office.

The new president's energetic and forceful leadership, which lasted from 1901 to 1909, gave the decade still another nickname: the Roosevelt era. To many historians and Americans in general, Teddy Roosevelt was the single most important person in the nation during the 1900s.

Roosevelt had already acquired a reputation as a ferocious enemy of political corruption. Despite the new president's assurances that he would not rock the boat with radical new policies, many veteran politicians feared the headstrong young man's ascent to power. Mark Hanna, the influential Ohio senator who had engineered McKinley's election, lamented, "Now look, that damned cowboy is President of the United States."[4]

Setting the Stage for the Century

The 1900s—the Age of Optimism, the Age of Confidence, the Roosevelt era— was, in many ways, a vastly significant period in American history. The changes that occurred during it set the tone for many crucial events and policies that evolved later in the century.

A massive wave of immigrants arrived in America, bringing with them not only a willingness to join a growing labor pool but also a variety of new cultural influences. For the first time, America aggressively moved to become a world power, a position it has kept ever since.

Aided by Roosevelt, an ardent conservationist, efforts to protect the nation's parks, game preserves, and wilderness became significantly stronger. There were intense efforts to clean up corrupt government and dubious business practices. Other controversial issues, such as conflicts between labor and industry, were addressed by the federal government for the first time in the nation's history.

On the home front, changes in technology dramatically transformed daily life. The rise of the automobile, for instance, changed the way Americans travel and radically altered the nation's landscape. Other new inventions, such as the vacuum cleaner, began making everyday life a little easier. Furthermore, new forms of art and entertainment (including a fabulous new medium called the motion picture) were thrilling audiences across the country. It was an exciting and fast-moving time.

People stroll the Coney Island boardwalk in New York around the turn of the century.

Daily Life: In the Good Old Summertime

Daily life for Americans of the 1900s was remarkably different from life today. Clothing styles, eating habits, entertainment, health concerns—nearly every aspect of life was not what it would be in later decades.

For one thing, there was a dramatic contrast between the rich upper class and the rest of society. Such differences were nothing new, and they continue to this day. However, the gap was even greater in the 1900s than today.

Steel manufacturer Andrew Carnegie was one of the very richest. At a time when the national income average was $500, Carnegie's personal income was $10 million annually. Carnegie and a handful of other wealthy men, primarily financiers and manufacturers, controlled nearly all of the nation's money. According to historians Dorothy and Carl J. Schneider, "At the turn of the century, 1 percent of the population owned more of the wealth than the other 99 percent."[5]

The richest and most socially prominent families were known as the "Four Hundred." The term was coined by a socialite who remarked that it was appropriate that the ballroom of the wealthy Astor family held only four hundred people—because there were only four hundred people "worth inviting."

Some wealthy families felt an obligation to help their fellow citizens by establishing philanthropic foundations; Carnegie, for instance, eventually gave much of his fortune away. Many, however, preferred to spend their fortunes on themselves. Their lives revolved around huge mansions, dozens of servants, lavish country homes, and a parade of overseas trips, balls, concerts, and dinners. Writer Walter Lord observes that lavish spending was not often considered to be in poor taste, and that less wealthy families often enjoyed hearing about the lives of the rich:

These were the days before taxes and high living costs. Nor were

Andrew Carnegie had a personal income of $10 million a year at a time when the average American made $500 a year.

there any brakes on the desire to spend. . . . For the most part, the privileged poured their money into projects that amused or interested them, while the not-so-privileged watched the splash.[6]

How the Four Hundred Lived

New York's Fifth Avenue was known as the "Gold Coast" because of its outrageous mansions built by the wealthy. The Vanderbilt family alone had seven mansions within seven blocks of the street, and others, including the Vanderbilts, Astors, Goulds, and Morgans, also owned houses there.

The Four Hundred, as the wealthiest New Yorkers were known, often had summer "cottages" as well. George Vanderbilt's North Carolina summer home, Breakers, boasted forty bedrooms, a library with 250,000 volumes, and over two hundred square miles of land. More men were employed tending the forests around Breakers than in the United States' entire forestry program.

Working and Middle Classes

Only a privileged few, of course, could indulge in the extravagances of the wealthy.

The majority of Americans were working-class people who had to continually struggle to make ends meet. A minority of Americans, meanwhile, fell below the poverty line. Historian Frank Freidel notes, "A careful estimate in 1902 indicated that about one-eighth of the people, or a total of ten million, lived in poverty."[7]

In between the rich and these less fortunate groups was a growing middle class, for whom life was comfortable, if not lavish.

For the middle and working classes, salaries were low by today's standards. A typical university professor, for instance, earned $3,500 a year. In skilled trades such as bricklaying, railroad engineering, and plumbing, a man could make as much as $24 a week, or $1,248 a year.

A young woman clerking in a store might earn only five or six dollars a week. The average wage for an unskilled laborer, meanwhile, was about nine dollars a week.

At the same time, however, prices were low. Roast beef cost about fifteen cents a pound, milk was six cents a quart, and a good pair of men's shoes cost about two dollars. A full dinner in a restaurant might cost a quarter. The university professor's salary would have been enough for him to afford a medium-sized house, employ a few servants, and maintain his family in decent style.

Even if a family could afford part-time domestic help, maintaining a house was hard work for a middle-class housewife. Many still made their own clothes and bedding, grew and canned their own fruits and vegetables, or sold extra milk or eggs to supplement the family income. This was also true, of course, for working-class families.

Styles

Although many women still made their families' clothes, this was no longer a necessity. The influx of immigrants to America during the 1900s included a large number of tailors. Together with technological changes, such as improvements in textile mills, these tailors greatly expanded the clothing industry. By the end of the decade, almost anything could be bought ready-made.

Fashions reflected the era's generally conservative outlook. Women's skirts always came down to the ground, even for such "unladylike" activities as bicycling or farm work. Tiny waists, achieved with a whalebone corset, were in style. Shoes were high and buttoned; hats were festooned with decorations like ostrich plumes and even stuffed birds.

Men's suits were almost always dark and heavy. For summers in the

Women work at a boot and shoe factory in 1908. They were part of a growing clothing industry that made it possible for people to buy most clothing ready-made.

country a man might wear white flannel, but there was no such thing as a summer-weight suit. Shirts had high, stiff collars and cuffs, detachable for easier cleaning.

No matter what a man did for a living, furthermore, a hat was necessary. Working-class men wore flat caps, farmers wore straw hats, middle-class men wore derbies, and professional men and the wealthy wore silk hats. Writer Frederick Lewis Allen notes, "To go hatless, except in the wide open spaces, was for the well-dressed male unthinkable."[8]

In the Home

Compared with today, housewives and servants in 1900 had relatively few labor-saving devices.

Running water, bathtubs, and indoor toilets were luxuries common only in wealthy houses. Most people washed with basins in their rooms and used outdoor privies. A metal bathtub might be hauled out once a week. Water was carried from a well or a faucet in the yard.

The kitchen stove sometimes also provided a home's only heat. Kitchen stoves and furnaces still used coal or wood, although gas was slowly becoming available. Refrigerators were not yet available, although some houses had iceboxes, which required regular supplies of ice. A few homes were lit with electricity, but most still used kerosene or gas.

Counteracting these inconveniences, dozens of wondrous new gadgets came on the market during the 1900s. Europeans excelled at pure scientific research, but American inventors easily outdistanced them in making practical use of technology.

Among the devices Americans perfected as more and more houses became wired for electricity were the following: electric toasters, electric irons, vacuum cleaners, single-unit washing machines, and hot water heaters. Other innovations included the safety razor, which eliminated the dangers of shaving with an old-fashioned straight razor by shielding the blade, and the Brownie, the first truly portable and easily operated camera. During the 1900s, American inventors also made crucial contributions to wireless broadcasting, leading to the radio revolution of future decades.

Americans not only knew how to make these things; they also had a knack for selling them. America's vast advertising industry received a tremendous boost with the consumer products of the 1900s, which introduced millions of eager buyers to the delights of new products via such catchy slogans as "Watch the Fords Go By" and "His Master's Voice" (for Victrola phonographs).

Electric Nation

Electricity had been used for industry for some time, but during the 1900s this use skyrocketed. In 1899 electricity ran only 5 percent of America's manufacturing machinery; by 1919, it ran 55 percent.

Electricity had an equally dramatic impact on daily life. Thanks to hundreds of new dams and generators, as well as technical improvements such as the perfection of mass-produced light bulbs, electric power became so cheap and reliable that its use multiplied a thousandfold in just a few years.

Electric streetcars and railroads became common in urban centers, replacing horse-drawn vehicles. Since safe and reliable electrically operated elevators were possible, increasingly taller buildings became possible as well.

Perhaps the most striking example of a practical application of electricity, however, was the telephone. In 1900 only a million and a half phones existed in the whole country, mostly for businesses and wealthy homes. By 1915, however, thanks to technical improvements that made phones cheaper and easier to use, the number had jumped to 9 million. Writer Fon Boardman Jr. wryly remarks, "The United States was on its way to being the talkingest nation in the world."[9]

Diet

The average family at the turn of the century ate relatively poorly compared

Electricity became widespread during the 1900s, allowing more people to have electric power in their homes. This allowed them to utilize the new invention of the telephone.

with its counterpart today. The range of foods from around the world now available in supermarkets would have been an unimaginable luxury even for the wealthiest family.

Railroads had begun experimenting with refrigerator cars, but they were not commonly used. Fresh fruits and vegetables were therefore generally unavailable during winter. A typical urban family's diet was a routine of bread, meat, salted fish, cheese, canned goods, and macaroni, supplemented with canned produce from a home garden. Poor country people often had to subsist on cornmeal mush, bacon, and game and fish they caught themselves.

In summer, fresh fruit and vegetables were more plentiful. Supplying food for the table was still a chore, however. Most food stores were small and independently owned, and they usually specialized. A typical shopping trip for a housewife might involve stops at a butcher, a fishmonger, an egg man, a milkman, and a "provisioner" (for produce). Chain stores, offering greater variety, consistent quality, and uniform pricing, would not become widespread until future decades.

Newspapers

An important part of everyday life for many Americans in the days before television and radio was the newspaper.

The 1900s saw a dramatic increase in the number and variety of newspapers. In 1899, there were 1,610 daily papers, but by 1909, that figure had grown

The Rise of Advertising

In the 1900s, advances in mass production caused a major shift in what Americans bought—and in the way they bought it. Mass production increased the overall number of consumer goods while lowering their individual prices. Also, technological breakthroughs allowed dozens of new gadgets to appear for the first time, from automobiles and typewriters to "talking machines" (gramophones), corsets, and breakfast foods. At the same time, the market for these products was expanding, thanks to the country's growing population and a rising national income.

Because of this increase in buying power, the 1900s also witnessed a strong rise in advertising, as manufacturers and ad agencies became increasingly sophisticated at convincing the public that it needed the new gadgets. The advertisers' primary tool was to announce a product in the popular magazines of the day, which represented the first time they could cheaply reach a broad-based, national audience.

One measure of their success was the growth in advertising revenue for one of the era's most popular magazines, the *Saturday Evening Post.* In 1902 the five-cent *Post* brought in just over $360,000 in advertising revenue. By 1922 that figure had increased to some $29 million—about eighty times the 1902 number.

Along with the increased number of new products came an increase in the number and size of advertising agencies. Some of the catchphrases invented by these agencies' copywriters proved so popular that they are still familiar today: "A Skin You Love to Touch" (Woodbury Soap); "Watch the Fords Go By"; "His Master's Voice" (Victrola); and "Milk from Contented Cows" (Darigold).

of copies sold—jumped from about 3 million to over 24 million, an increase of eightfold. By comparison, the population of the country increased by a much smaller percentage, from about 76 million to about 92 million.

One way that newspapers increased circulation was by featuring sensational stories about brutal murders and juicy divorces. This was called yellow journalism, probably because cheap and sensational books had once been wrapped in yellow jackets. Chief among the yellow publishers were William Randolph Hearst and Joseph Pulitzer, whose newspapers had reported rabble-rousing pieces on the Spanish-American War late in the previous century.

As a way of further increasing circulation, newspapers also began introducing features, that is, items that were not "hard" news. These included comic strips, recipes, humor, puzzles, bedtime stories for children, and advice to the lovelorn. "Mutt and Jeff," the first daily comic strip to feature recurring characters, appeared in 1909 in the *San Francisco Examiner.*

A newsboy proclaims the latest headlines to passersby in hopes of selling his newspapers. Newspaper reporters used sensational headlines and stories, called yellow journalism, to entice readers and increase circulation.

to 2,600. During that same period, overall daily circulation—that is, the number

Entertainment

In the 1900s, before TV, radio, or feature films, people watched live entertainment or made their own.

Children played with simple toys, often homemade, such as dolls, kites, mumblety-peg, roller skates, bicycles, and marbles. On weekends, families took part in church functions like ice-cream socials. State fairs also provided an opportunity for families to get away and sample exotic new experiences.

Playing music at home was a favorite pastime; the 1905 Sears mail-order catalog devoted sixty pages just to musical instruments. Most cities and many small towns boasted amateur orchestras.

Pianos were popular items, and every respectable middle-class or upper-class house had one. If no one in the family could play, they could rely on the mechanical or player piano, which used punched-paper rolls, and the gramophone.

People regularly gathered around the piano in the evening to sing popular or religious songs. Sales of sheet music for the piano were huge: 2 billion copies just in the year 1910. The most popular songs of the day were usually sentimental ("Sweet Adeline," "By the Light of the Silvery Moon," "Shine on, Harvest Moon"), patriotic ("You're a Grand Old Flag"), or nostalgic ("Schooldays," "In the Good Old Summertime").

Music and Dance

Recorded music was just coming into its own in the 1900s. Edison's invention of the cylinder phonograph had already swept the country, but during the 1900s this marvel was considerably improved and refined, especially by the new Victor Talking Machine, which played flat disks instead of cylinders. These disks sound hopelessly tinny and scratchy by today's standards, but in their day they were dazzling.

Classical music was popular, and people avidly listened to recordings of famous musicians like singer Enrico Caruso. In large cities, music fans could gather at the local opera house to hear their favorites.

Jazz would not take the nation by storm until the next decade. However, two of its predecessors, blues and ragtime, were popular forms of music during the 1900s. A crucial piece in the early development of recorded blues, Jelly Roll Morton's "New Orleans Blues," was published in 1902.

Another popular musical style was ragtime, a syncopated piano-based style that African-American composers such as Scott Joplin brought to a fine art. Ragtime flourished during the decade in the black community, but it was ignored by the public until 1911, when the gifted songwriter Irving Berlin wrote a hit song, "Alexander's Ragtime Band," which is still a standard.

Ragtime was based on one of the many popular dance styles of the day; others included the turkey trot and the cakewalk. Modern "serious" dance also made some important advances in the 1900s. In particular, the pioneering husband-and-wife team of Ted Shawn and Ruth St. Denis, and the equally innovative Isadora Duncan, created some of their most important works during the decade.

Best-Sellers 1900–1910

One million or more copies of the following books were sold during the first decade of the twentieth century. They are listed in descending order of sales.

Title	Author	Year Published
The Wonderful Wizard of Oz	L. Frank Baum	1900
The Story of the Bible	Jessy Lyman Hurlburt	1904
Freckles	Gene Stratton Porter	1904
The Virginian	Owen Wister	1902
The Trail of the Lonesome Pine	John Fox Jr.	1908
The Crisis	Winston Churchill	1901
Daily Strength for Daily Needs	Mary W. Tileston	1901
The Shepherd of the Hills	Harold Bell Wright	1907
Appleton's English-Spanish, Spanish-English Dictionary	Arturo Cuyas	1903
The Little Shepherd of Kingdom Come	John Fox Jr.	1903
The Rosary	Florence Barclay	1910
The Simple Life	Charles Wagner	1901

Source: Alyce Payne Hackett, *70 Years of Best Sellers 1895–1965*, (New York & London, 1967), 12–30.

Books

The number of books Americans read for pleasure increased enormously in the 1900s. Before 1898, few books sold more than 100,000 copies; during the first decade of the century, sales figures in that range became commonplace. In part, this was due to rapidly improving education and literacy. Another factor was the desire for self-improvement that was part of the era's atmosphere.

Best-selling books of the decade ranged from uplifting religious tracts to sentimental novels like *Rebecca of Sun-nybrook Farm* and thrilling adventure tales like Jack London's *Call of the Wild*. Millions of readers also eagerly followed the daring exploits of the upstanding heroes and heroines found in "dime novels." L. Frank Baum's enduring series of books about the Wizard of Oz, the first of which appeared in 1900, also proved hugely popular.

Historical and western novels were best-sellers as well. *The Virginian* popularized the phrase "smile when you say that" and did much to shape the romantic ideal of the cowboy. One of the decade's most important literary novels, Theodore Dreiser's *Sister Carrie*, was first published in 1900. However, the publisher's wife was so shocked at its frank depiction of sexuality that the book was suppressed for over a decade.

Traveling Shows and Trolley Parks

Traveling shows were another important form of entertainment. Dozens of circuses crisscrossed the country, each using as many as ninety railroad cars to transport their setups from place to place. In a small town, the arrival of the circus was one of the most exciting events of the year.

Chautauquas, traveling shows that set up in theaters or portable tents, offered mixtures of light entertainment and serious educational speakers. Many famous people appeared on the chautauqua circuit, including Mark Twain, presidential candidate William Jennings Bryan, and actress Sarah Bernhardt. Such celebrities often appeared on a bill alongside a variety of singers, magicians, dancers, and animal acts.

A traveling chautauqua visits a small town. Such infrequent events might be the only entertainment people in a small town might see for a year or more.

St. Louis Exposition

"Meet me in St. Louis, Louis, Meet me at the fair . . ." was a popular song in the summer of 1904. The subject was the Louisiana Purchase Exposition, held that year in St. Louis, Missouri.

Like many fairs, the St. Louis fair highlighted technology and progress. Among the marvels on display: cooking by electricity, one hundred automobiles, electric hearing aids, and "house cleaning done by pneumatic process without removing the carpets"—that is, vacuum cleaning.

Another of the fair's themes concerned Pacific countries. In particular, buildings devoted to the Philippine Islands gave Americans glimpses of life in a country newly acquired by the United States.

Not everything was strictly educational. A huge Ferris wheel thrilled thousands. The third Olympic Games were held alongside the fair. The hamburger and iced tea first gained widespread popularity there. A third food novelty, the ice cream cone, was invented when the owner of an ice cream booth ran out of serving bowls and improvised with waffles.

The largest Ferris wheel (340 feet high) was included in the St. Louis World's Fair in 1904.

Vaudeville was related to the chatauqua. Chains of vaudeville theaters featured nonstop shows of singers, dancers, musicians, magicians, and actors. Many performers who later found fame in the movies, including Buster Keaton, the Marx Brothers, and W. C. Fields, started as vaudevillians. The life of a traveling showman was rough; veterans half-jokingly divided the territory they traveled around into the Bed Bug Belt, the Cyclone Belt, the Broiling Belt, and the Hellish Hotel Belt.

One form of entertainment that the public traveled to see, instead of the other way around, was the trolley park. Trolley parks were amusement parks, built at the edges of cities by streetcar companies, that featured diversions such as Ferris wheels, band concerts, baseball games, and ponds for boating and bathing. An added attraction of the trolley cars themselves during summer, in the days before air-conditioning, were the breezes that blew in and out of the cars as they rattled along, cooling off weary and overheated passengers en route.

Sports

In the 1900s football was popular at only a few Ivy League colleges, and basketball had yet to catch on. The upper classes preferred expensive amateur athletics, such as tennis, golf, horse racing, sailing, and polo.

Baseball, however, was already America's most popular sport and was fast on its way to becoming a national obsession.

Amateur baseball teams had existed for decades. By the 1900s, every small town had a fiercely competitive amateur league. Newspaper editor William Allen White recalls the keen attention to the sport in his hometown of Emporia, Kansas:

Of a late summer afternoon, the town gathered at these games with noisy loyalty and great excitement, the women in their best big hats and high sleeves and wide skirts, the men in . . . tailless shirts gathered with a rubber string under the waist just inside and below the trouser top—quite fashionable and exciting.[10]

Professional teams, meanwhile, had been active since the 1880s, and during the 1900s commercial baseball's popularity soared. In 1902, professional teams had an annual overall audience of 3.5 million; by 1911, that number had nearly doubled to 6.5 million. The American League was established in 1900 to rival the National League to organize new teams. The rival leagues played the first World Series in 1903, with Boston emerging victorious over Pittsburgh.

In 1903, the first "baseball palace" was built in Pittsburgh, followed soon by similar stadiums in Chicago, Cleveland, Boston, and New York. The sport's most enduring anthem, "Take Me Out to the Ball Game," was first heard in 1909.

The Flicks

Perhaps the most important development in popular entertainment during the decade was the birth of the movie industry.

Thomas Edison had already invented a method of projecting moving pictures on a screen. His process, known by trade names such as Kinetoscope and Vitagraph, was already being used to make short films for vaudeville shows.

But these flicks, which featured melodramatic titles like *The Face on the Barroom Floor* and *The Curse of Drink*, were brief vignettes with no story lines. Some were no more than thrilling shots of far-off wonders like the Grand Canyon.

The first decade of the century saw a dramatic improvement in the quality and length of these primitive "flicks."

The Early Film Industry

Beginning in the 1900s, an improbable group became the foremost entrepreneurs of a new form of art and entertainment: the movies.

Jewish immigrants from eastern Europe began to dominate the early movie industry. They turned Hollywood into the film world's center, established major studios like Metro-Goldwyn-Mayer and Universal, and created the production systems used for decades to make movies.

Though motivated by profit, they also expanded the creative possibilities of what most people considered only a crude novelty. Under their guidance, movies became longer and more complex, directors were encouraged (to a degree, at least) to be innovative, and well-known actors and actresses were lured from the "legitimate" stage.

Among the most important of these men was studio magnate Adolph Zukor, who had come to the United States as a fifteen-year-old orphan. A furrier by trade, Zukor became interested in movies and founded a chain of theaters.

Another immigrant, Samuel Goldfish (who later changed his name to Goldwyn), had come from Poland at the age of twelve. He worked as a glove salesman before forming a film company with his brother-in-law, Jesse Lasky, and an actor turned director, Cecil B. DeMille. A merger between this company and Zukor's became one of the first film studios to rival the early Edison studio, and was soon turning out dozens of hits.

Zukor and Goldwyn's principal rival was yet another immigrant, Lewis J. Zeleznick, who later changed his name to Selznick. After coming to America at age twelve and failing as a jeweler, Selznick turned a small film studio, Universal, into a major corporation. Selznick, the stereotypical Hollywood producer, collected Ming vases, maintained a fleet of Rolls-Royces, and enjoyed entertaining starlets in his lavish homes. His son, David O. Selznick, continued the tradition.

Of these men and their colleagues, historian Page Smith writes in *America Enters the World*, "Of all the odd and exotic moments in the nation's history there was none stranger than the conjunction of Thomas Edison's moving picture machine and the exotic company of Jewish immigrants from Russia, Poland and Latvia waiting . . . to be the purveyors of America's dreams and, as it would turn out, the world's dreams as well."

The first true narrative film—that is, a movie that told a complete story—was a twelve-minute epic, *The Great Train Robbery*. Released in 1903, it marked a milestone in the development of this enduringly popular entertainment.

All through the 1900s, theaters sprang up across the country to show a constantly changing, increasingly sophisticated array of movies. Sometimes these theaters were quite elaborate, and sometimes they were merely an empty hall with folding chairs.

They were called nickelodeons because the entrance fee was a nickel. The first nickelodeon opened in 1902 in Los Angeles, a small town that would soon be transformed by the new movie industry. By 1908, there were an estimated ten thousand nickelodeons nationwide.

For many years, however, serious theater directors and actors scorned the movies. The flicks were considered by many to be simple-minded fads that would soon go away. No one believed that they would ever rival "legitimate"

An early movie theater, or nickelodeon, circa 1900. The nickelodeon's popularity put a dent in stage entertainment ticket sales.

theater. Historian Frank Freidel writes, "At first . . . the idea of the motion picture offering serious competition to the stage appeared ludicrous."[11]

Changes

The decade saw changes in many areas, such as entertainment and technology. These new inventions created a feeling, at least in urban centers, that America was in constant motion. Frederic Harrison, a visiting Englishman, noted this when he wrote, "Life in the States is one perpetual whirl of telephones, telegrams, phonographs, electric bells, motors, lifts, and automatic instruments."[12]

Despite these innovations, however, the lives of many Americans—including immigrants, children, and farm laborers—remained desperately hard. During the decade, citizens and government authorities began a series of sweeping social reforms, generally called Progressivism, that sought to make life easier for these people.

Chapter Two

European immigrants crowd the deck of a transatlantic ship as it arrives in New York Harbor in 1906. The arrival of hundreds of thousands of immigrants in the 1900s created new problems and opportunities for the United States.

Social Problems, Social Cures: The Birth of the Square Deal

As the United States transformed it-self into an industrialized country in the nineteenth century, a number of problems emerged. These still lingered as the new century began.

Many of these problems had been created by the overwhelming crowds of people who flocked to cities in search of jobs. Some of these people came from rural parts of America; to a larger degree, they were immigrants from overseas.

Since city-run services, such as sewer systems and police departments, were often inadequate for handling large groups of people, disease and crime grew worse. Also, the need to house poor working families quickly, combined with a lack of stringent building and health codes, led to the creation of decrepit urban slums.

These and other problems were seen by social activists of the era as interrelated injustices. Among the other wrongs identified during the 1900s were unethical business practices, corrupt government, and the lack of unemployment insurance and safety laws for workers. Still others included inadequacies in civil rights, child labor laws, access to birth control, and the prohibition of alcohol.

Progressivism

One of the defining characteristics of the 1900s was a wide-ranging social reform movement that tried to fight these problems efficiently and effectively. There were many separate efforts, with many different goals, within one movement. Historians often loosely group these diverse efforts together as the Progressive movement. This era lasted roughly from just before the turn of the century to the beginning of World War I.

Reformers in the 1900s were known generally as Progressivists. Most came from the middle class. They typi-

A Notorious Murder

Perhaps the most notorious murder case of the era involved a feud between two wealthy men. It was eagerly followed by people from every class, who read about its latest developments in the "yellow" press as well as in the more reputable newspapers.

Harry K. Thaw was a rich playboy, already infamous for antics like wrecking cafes and riding a horse up the steps of an exclusive New York club. He became obsessed by the fact that his wife, a former chorus girl named Evelyn Nesbit, had once had an affair with Stanford White, the country's most prominent architect. He was convinced, perhaps correctly, that White was still pressing his attentions on her. In June of 1906, Thaw shot White dead in the roof-garden theater at Madison Square Garden, a building White himself had designed.

At Thaw's first trial, the jury could not reach a verdict. Found not guilty by reason of insanity at his second trial, Thaw was sent to a mental institution. He later escaped, was recaptured in Canada, and in 1915 was declared sane and released.

cally believed in capitalism and in democracy, and did not want to upset it. However, they also felt strongly that human nature could be changed for the better with proper upbringing, environment, and education. They therefore believed that measures such as better schooling and increasingly strict laws would be enough to right the wrongs they observed.

Others argued for more basic political change. Coming primarily from the ranks of the working class and the poor, they argued that America's problems were caused by capitalism. Only with new economic and political systems, such as socialism, could necessary changes be made.

A handful of reformers, meanwhile, came from the wealthy class. Steel baron Andrew Carnegie, for instance, donated some $350 million between 1901 and 1919 to worthy causes, including money for the libraries that bear his name. Carnegie believed that such philanthropy was a way toward social betterment and improving the nation as a whole.

Overall, Progressive reformers yearned to make over society into a purer, more benign form. Many saw their work as a moral, family-oriented, humane, and even religious crusade. They sought to return America to essentially conservative, rural values in the light of the rapid changes brought on by industrialization. Historian Richard Hofstadter comments, "Progressivism, at its heart, was an effort to realize familiar and traditional ideals under novel circumstances."[13]

The Square Deal

Theodore Roosevelt was the movement's spearhead and chief spokesman. To millions of Americans, in fact, Roosevelt and Progressivism were virtually synonymous.

As governor of New York, he had been a tireless champion of reform. As president, he immediately made it clear that he would continue in the same vein. During his first annual message to Congress, delivered shortly after he took office, he stated:

> The tremendous and highly complex industrial development which went on with ever-accelerated rapidity during the latter half of the nineteenth century brings us face to face at the beginning of the twentieth century with very serious social problems. The old laws, and the old customs . . . are no longer sufficient.[14]

Roosevelt was a superb politician, and he was able to synthesize the various goals of Progressive reformers into what seemed, at times, to be a single movement. Borrowing a phrase from journalist Lincoln Steffens, Roosevelt called his strategy the Square Deal. Every American, Roosevelt declared, deserved a square deal—and he was going to fight to make sure that every American got it.

Some historians have criticized Roosevelt for not doing enough, for compromising too much to please various factions. Nonetheless, they acknowledge

Theodore Roosevelt inspires Americans with a moving speech. Perhaps one of Roosevelt's most important contributions was to instill in ordinary Americans a desire to improve society.

Perhaps Roosevelt's most important contribution to the movement was simply to inspire in the average American a desire for social change. He fervently believed that every American needed to be involved, and he was brilliant at instilling that belief in others. In a 1901 magazine article, Roosevelt wrote, "No hard-and-fast rule can be laid down as to the way in which such work [reform] must be done; but most certainly every man, whatever his position, should strive to do it in some way and to some degree."[15]

The Muckrakers

The Progressives were aided in their crusades by a number of journalists. Writers who document social, political, and economic ills are today usually called investigative reporters. In the 1900s, however, the term "muckraker" was used.

The most famous muckraking magazine was *McClure's*, which started the movement in earnest by publishing

that his ability to popularize the movement was invaluable.

three explosive exposés: a detailed history of Standard Oil by Ida Tarbell that laid bare the company's unethical business practices, a series by Lincoln Steffens on political corruption in large cities, and an article by Ray Stannard Baker about a bitter coal strike that strongly criticized the striking union. Muckraking began to attract notice in 1902 and reached a peak of popularity in 1906, by which time millions of readers faithfully followed "the literature of exposure."

Besides the journalists who worked for *McClure's*, many other writers also published influential books and articles condemning social evils. Frank Norris's novel *The Octopus* (1901) painted a vivid portrait of California ranchers battling railroad corporations. Upton Sinclair's novel *The Jungle* (1906) exposed terrible practices in the meatpacking industry. Many newspapers, notably the *New York World* and the *Kansas City Star,* also published influential articles by crusading journalists.

The term "muckraking" came from Teddy Roosevelt. He appreciated the efforts of investigative journalists, but he sometimes felt that they went too far. Shortly after the appearance of an investigative article attacking the U.S. Senate, Roosevelt complained in a speech that the article's author was like the man in John Bunyan's seventeenth-

Upton Sinclair's exposé of the meatpacking industry, The Jungle, *was just one of several works that were part of a movement called "muckraking."*

century book *The Pilgrim's Progress*, who concentrated so much on clearing mud with a "muckrake" that he never looked up to notice anything worthy: "The men with the muckrakes are often indispensable to the well-being of society," Roosevelt declared, "but only when they know when to stop raking the muck and [look up] to the crown of worthy endeavor."[16]

On the whole, however, muckraking journalists and the president were in tune with each other. The journalists echoed Roosevelt's belief that the American public needed to take action and accept responsibility when confronted with injustice. The publisher of *Mc-Clure's* wrote:

Capitalists, workingmen, politicians, citizens—all breaking the law, or letting it be broken. Who is left to uphold it? . . . There is no one left; none but all of us. . . . We are all doing our worst and making the public pay. . . . We have to pay in the end, every one of us.[17]

Tenements

One of the most serious urban problems that reformers attacked was the terrible condition of housing.

At the turn of the century, city governments were under no obligation to build inexpensive public housing for needy families. Also, there were no standards for building and maintaining safe, clean housing.

As a result, nearly every medium or large city in America had slum neighborhoods of cheap, quickly constructed apartment buildings. These so-called tenements were overcrowded, dirty, and dangerous. Many were "dumbbell" buildings, named for the way their apartments

were arranged around a central airshaft. This airshaft provided direct light and fresh air for only four of the fourteen rooms on each floor.

Dumbbell-type or not, tenement buildings were so overcrowded that as many as four thousand people were sometimes squeezed into a single block. Typical of the condition of such slums were the buildings found by a committee of architects in Boston in 1899, which reported

dirty and battered walls and ceilings, dark cellars with water standing in them, alleys littered with garbage and filth, broken and leaking drain-pipes . . . dark and filthy

A woman strings beads in her tiny tenement apartment. This woman is lucky, however, because, although small, her room is unshared.

water-closets, closets long frozen or otherwise out of order . . . and houses so dilapidated and so much settled [on their foundations] that they are dangerous.[18]

Fixing the Slums

As reform-minded activists took on the task of cleaning up tenements, conditions slowly improved.

In this work, Progressive reformers built on the work of earlier activists, such as the pioneering photographer and investigative journalist, Jacob Riis. In 1890, Riis had published a book, *How the Other Half Lives*, that graphically exposed the horrifying conditions under which tenement dwellers were forced to live. Ten years later, Riis was able to report some improvement since the publication of his groundbreaking book, but much was left to be done.

Reform-minded legislation was passed in many cities throughout the decade. A Tenement House Commission was established to study the problem in New York City, where the most notorious slums were located. The following year, laws were passed that toughened housing standards in the city.

Other reforms elsewhere included similar changes in building codes and housing requirements. These new laws called for stiff penalties if builders and

owners did not provide basic amenities such as running water, improved sanitation, larger rooms, limits on maximum occupancy, and fire protection. By 1910, many slumlords had improved the conditions of existing buildings, and new construction was also on the upswing. While far from ideal, the situation regarding tenement buildings had vastly improved.

Immigrants

Tenement dwellers were typically those who could afford nothing better, and many such people were recent immigrants.

America is a nation of immigrants, and since its founding there have been regular waves of new arrivals. By 1900, one-third of the people in the United States were foreign-born immigrants or first-generation children of foreign-born immigrants. Furthermore, the decade 1900–1909 saw a record number of new arrivals. During those years, 8,796,000 people arrived in search of a better life, more than in any other decade before or since.

This enormous wave of immigration had a major impact on the way America developed. New customs, manners, languages, food, religious practices, and cultures flooded the country as never before. However, it also created a number of tough problems.

Progressive reformers found much to do involving the immigrants. Many Progressives were especially interested in supporting the Americanization of newcomers, teaching them English, civics, and other tools that would help them find better jobs.

Some immigrants resented what they felt was a patronizing attitude on the part of reformers, most of whom were Anglo-Saxon Protestants. However, many others were grateful for the help. For them, the American dream included the process of assimilation, that is, of becoming Americanized. Learning English and embracing new ways, they realized, was an effective way to break away from the slums.

They were eager to abandon their old ways of dressing, to speak English without an accent, to acquire American friends and manners. One Polish immigrant, frustrated over finding work only in a Polish enclave in Massachusetts, expressed this feeling in a letter written in broken English to the state's Commission on Immigration:

> I want live with american people, but where? Not in the country, because I want go in the city, free evening schools and lern. I'm looking for help. If somebody could give me another job between american people, help me live with them and lern english—and could tell me the best way how I can lern—it would be very, very good for me.[19]

Ethnic Tension

The influx of immigrants also created tensions among various ethnic groups. Earlier immigrant groups, notably the Irish, German, and Scandinavians, were relatively well established by 1900. The vast majority of the newer immigrants, however, were not from these already-established groups. They were mostly Italians, Slavs, Greeks, Poles, and Jews from southern and eastern Europe.

Especially in big cities, these fresh immigrants and their families often

Immigration to the United States 1900–1909

	1900–1909
Total in Millions	8.2
Percent of Total From:	
Ireland	4.2
Germany	4.0
United Kingdom	5.7
Scandinavia	5.9
Canada	1.5
Russia	18.3
Austria-Hungary	24.4
Italy	23.5

Source: David Ward, *Cities and Immigrants* (1971), 53.

outnumbered native-born and established immigrant groups. Poor new arrivals, usually speaking little or no English, they lived under harsh conditions and often had to be content with menial work: backbreaking unskilled jobs in factories, on the railroads, or in the garment trade.

The differences between "old" and "new" immigrants often led to tension. Established Americans feared the strange customs and religions of the new arrivals. They feared the relatively high birth rate among immigrants as compared with the low birth rate among

higher-income groups. They feared that jobs would be taken from them.

As a result, considerable prejudice existed against new arrivals. Sometimes this prejudice was within ethnic groups; established Jews from Germany and Holland, for instance, often looked down upon newly arrived Jews from eastern Europe. Even Theodore Roosevelt, a generally tolerant man, warned darkly against "race suicide," by which he meant the dilution and weakening of Anglo-Saxon Protestant stock.

Throughout the decade, there were attempts to stop the flood of new immi-

Immigrants from Antwerp, Belgium, sit on deck while bound for Ellis Island in 1901. During the 1900s, many of the customs and ideas of the new immigrants seemed strange and dangerous to natives.

grants, most of whom arrived through the famous port at Ellis Island in New York Harbor. Frank Freidel notes, "Many Americans, both conservative and progressive, were susceptible to the popular dogma [belief] of Anglo-Saxon superiority, and joined in the anti-immigration movement."[20]

Anti-Asian Feeling

Throughout the decade, anti-immigrationists succeeded in passing a series of laws excluding a wide range of undesirable groups ranging from ex-convicts to alcoholics.

The anti-immigration movement was most effective in excluding Asian populations. A federal law passed in 1902 effectively excluded Chinese workers, who had made up the vast majority of workers in western railroad and mining crews. The anti-immigrationists resented the flood of Chinese labor, since it took away jobs from workers they felt were more deserving.

People on the West Coast were also hostile toward the trickle of Japanese immigrants, fewer than a thousand each year. Their excitement was fueled by lurid articles about the "Yellow Peril" in newspapers such as those of

A WORD OF CAUTION TO OUR FRIENDS, THE CIGAR-MAKERS.
Through the smoke it is easy to see the approach of Chinese cheap labor.

This cartoon claims that Chinese immigrants will ultimately put native Americans out of work. These kinds of sentiments produced a legal backlash against Asian immigration.

the conservative Hearst chain. These stories, which played on diplomatic and political tensions already existing between America and Japan, warned that the "purity" of American society was being threatened by a small number of people with unfamiliar ways and looks.

In 1906 the San Francisco school board voted to segregate Japanese schoolchildren, even though there were only ninety-three Japanese students in the district. The Japanese government officially protested this and other anti-Japanese actions in America, and already tense feelings between the two nations increased. However, Roosevelt was able to work out a diplomatic compromise. He persuaded San Francisco to desegregate its schools, and in return he quietly consented to an informal "gentlemen's agreement" that allowed only a small number of Japanese agricultural laborers to enter the country.

Animosity and resentment still ran high. Historians Oscar Theodore Barck Jr. and Nelson Manfred Blake note, "Although Oriental immigration had never been large in comparison with European, it provoked a disproportionate clamor of opposition among jealous native workers."[21]

Education

Another problem facing social reformers was the quality of education in America. On the whole, literacy was fairly high compared with other countries; one survey at the time put it as high as 90 percent. Also, universal education—that is, the guarantee of free school for everyone—was already a mainstay in America.

Nonetheless, there were many problems. For one thing, public schools were under the control of local districts. There were virtually no federal or even statewide efforts to maintain standards. This meant that the quality and amount of education varied widely from area to area. As of 1900, for instance, only seven states required school attendance to the age of sixteen. Thanks to reformers, however, by 1910 the number of states with this requirement had increased to thirty-three.

The amount and quality of schooling changed over the decade in other ways. Kindergartens, once a rarity, spread rapidly. The number of public high schools nearly doubled between 1900 and 1914, and the number of students increased two and a half times.

The change was rapid. In 1900 the average elementary schoolchild attended a one-room school for only about half the current school year, and was taught by an undertrained, ill-paid teacher. By 1914, the average student attended more days during a longer school year, and was taught by a series of better-trained, better-paid teachers.

Frederick C. Howe, an activist and scholar, noted at the time that public libraries, which were becoming increasingly popular during the decade, played an especially important role in education by providing a chance for lifelong learning. He wrote, "Through them opportunity is offered for a continuation of

A nursery school in 1906 has children line up in an orderly circle. Formal education improved greatly throughout the 1900s.

study, even after the door of the school has closed."[22]

Corrupt Cities

In a number of cities, reformists also turned their attention to cleaning up corrupt politics. In these cities, the iron grip of so-called "machines," run by dishonest politicians, controlled a variety of interests.

These politicians became rich and powerful through their efforts. They were supported by businesses with a similar interest in maintaining the un-

ethical status quo and by civic employees whose favors could be bought for a price. For instance, the head of the commission controlling a city's building permits might be persuaded to look the other way when a shady deal was being put in place. Historian George Mowry elaborates:

> In New York, Jersey City, Chicago, St. Louis, and Minneapolis, and in San Francisco and Los Angeles, the tale read much the same: city councils for sale and mayors protecting criminals; water, gas, and

street-railway franchises granted for fifty years or more to private corporations with the legal right to charge exorbitant fees; police whose salaries were regularly enhanced by contributions from houses of prostitution and other noxious institutions.[23]

Supplying Votes

The votes needed to elect corrupt politicians and keep them in office were usually supplied by the poor and the working class, especially immigrants.

Machine politicians related to these groups in individual and personable ways, and they were generally extremely popular. The machines provided concrete benefits for these groups, who often were otherwise virtually powerless: the machine politicians saw that jobs, social services such as financial help during troubled times, and access to authority were forthcoming. In return, loyal voters guaranteed their votes on election day, and sometimes cheated at the ballot box to increase the odds. A joke of the day was that citizens were urged to "vote early and often."

The relationship between politician and voter was therefore often one of "I'll scratch your back and you scratch mine." One official of New York City's political machine summed it up this way:

This cartoon depicts a dishonest businessman, representative of a political machine, barring the way to public office. Political corruption was widespread during the 1900s.

If a family is burned out, I don't ask whether they are Republicans or Democrats. I just get quarters [lodging] for them, buy clothes for them if their clothes were burned up, and fix them up till they get things runnin' again. Who can tell how many votes these fires bring me?[24]

City Reforms

Such an attitude is not necessarily illegal, of course, but in practice it often skirted the boundaries of ethics.

Political bosses who controlled entire cities were naturally opposed to efforts toward reforming their personal fiefdoms. So were those interested in keeping the machines in power, such as saloonkeepers who stood to gain more from the bosses than from clean government.

Nonetheless, reform movements in many cities, particularly Toledo and Cleveland, were remarkably successful during the 1900s at cleaning out corrupt city government.

Once reform movements managed to unseat dishonest mayors, they often replaced them with city commissions. This form of government was easier to keep honest, in part because it divided the power among several top people instead of only one.

The city commission concept first took root in Galveston, Texas, in 1900, after a hurricane and tidal wave killed thousands and destroyed the city. The old methods of government broke down and a commission of five was appointed to enact laws and run the main city departments. The strategy worked so well that many other cities soon adopted it. By the end of the Progressive era, over four hundred cities were operating under similar commissions.

Change on the State Level

Political reform also occurred on the state level. Among the governors who rose to prominence on statewide reform measures were Robert ("Fighting Bob") LaFollette of Wisconsin, Hiram Johnson of California, and Woodrow Wilson of New Jersey, a future president. These men pledged to sweep out corruption not only in the governor's office but also in the legislatures, where bribery, illegal political deals, and kickbacks were commonplace.

One important method they used was the placement of initiatives and referendums on ballots at election time. This gave ordinary voters greater control over what measures were passed. The first use of initiatives and referendums was in Oregon in 1902; by 1918, twenty states had adopted them as a regular part of the political process.

Another important tool was the use of the direct primary. This gave voters the ability to eliminate the automatic choice of candidates put forward by political machines. The direct primary was first used in Mississippi in 1902, and by 1915 had been adopted in some form by every state in the union.

Foes of these measures complained that they forced voters to be "do-it-yourself legislators." Citizens generally liked having the added responsibility, however. They recognized that the added control usually resulted in cleaner, more efficient government. As historian Otis Pease notes, during the Progressive era "reformers everywhere were beginning to assert that the central issue of their time was to restore the power and the operations of the government to the control of the ordinary citizen."[25]

Health Conditions

By today's standards, health care at the turn of the century was dismal. Still another issue of concern to social reformers, therefore, was public health.

One measure of overall health care is the average lifespan. In America in 1900, men lived to be an average of forty-six and women forty-eight. This is in striking contrast to the life expectancy of Americans today, which is well over seventy-five for both males and females.

There were several reasons for the era's shortened lifespan, such as poor sanitation and pollution. Many people bathed only once a week, and disease-cultivating factors such as inadequate lavatory facilities and public spitting were common. Pollution was also rampant in industrial areas, and laborers in mines and factories were especially vulnerable to problems such as black lung disease.

Malnutrition was also rampant; the concept of eating certain foods to provide vitamins was not firmly established until later in the century. An even more pressing problem was that of rampant germs and bacteria; antibiotics had not yet been invented, so even a simple infection could easily prove fatal.

People in the 1900s, therefore, rarely lived long enough to be plagued by diseases associated with aging, such as heart attacks or Alzheimer's disease. Instead, they typically died of maladies that are today generally treatable with antibiotics, such as tuberculosis, pneumonia, malaria, diphtheria, and influenza.

Better Health

Reformers zealously promoted improvements in the nation's health. One change during the 1900s placed a greater burden on hospitals, nurses, and physicians.

In the previous century, housewives had traditionally taken on health care, and cookbooks often included recipes for medicines. During the 1900s, however, nursing the seriously ill increasingly became a task for professionals.

Surgeons train other doctors as they operate in a hospital in 1900. Many reformers took a great interest in public health, helping to lower the mortality rate during the decade.

tional Tuberculosis Association, founded in 1904, raised money to fund research and treatment of these hazards.

Various government programs also helped improve the overall health picture. A program to exterminate mosquitoes in tropical U.S. territories effectively eliminated yellow fever. And a parasite called hookworm, the cause of a debilitating disease prevalent in the Midwest and South, was also virtually eliminated, thanks to a program sponsored by the Rockefeller Foundation that began in the 1900s.

As a result, between 1900 and 1920 the number of hospital beds doubled. Training for America's doctors and nurses, which had been generally lax, was made more stringent. Progress was also made in creating new therapies to battle various serious threats; citizens' organizations such as the Na-

Pure Food and Drug

Reform in health issues was also addressed through the passage of several laws regulating food and drug manufacturing.

As of 1900 there was little protection for the consumer from unsanitary or harmful foods and drugs. Many dangerous preservatives and adulterants were routinely used. Meat and milk were often processed and sold under dirty conditions. Patent medicines were alleged to be cures for anything from tuberculosis to cancer, when in fact they were usually little more than colored water, a bitter flavor, and a lacing of alcohol.

Much of this unregulated trade in dangerous food and so-called health cures changed with the passage of the most important federal health law of the 1900s, the Pure Food and Drug Act of 1906. This law established strict guidelines for the safe preparation of a variety of foods and medicines. Among other things, it authorized the government to send inspectors into food-related manufacturers and restaurants to ensure cleanliness and purity.

A related federal law also served to enforce meat inspection. Other operations guaranteed, on state and regional levels, such preventative health measures as pasteurization of milk and the chlorination of water supplies.

Temperance

Some reformers focused their energy on an issue they considered the single greatest source of moral decay in America—the consumption of alcohol.

Alcoholism was indeed a serious problem for many. The United States in its rougher frontier days had gained a reputation for being home to many hard drinkers, and even into the industrial era the hard lives of factory workers drove many in the new urban lower classes to drink. Neighborhood taverns had become symbols of public drunkenness, vice, and degeneracy.

The best-known antialcohol organizations, supported mainly by conservative Protestants, were the Women's Christian Temperance Union (WCTU) and the Anti-Saloon League, both founded in the previous century. They led public demonstrations and campaigns, such as the formation of special groups of young women who promised to marry only men who abstained from alcohol. Their motto was, "Lips that touch liquor shall never touch mine."

The most famous of these antialcohol activists was Carry Nation, a formidable six-foot-tall Kansas woman whose method was direct and effective: she walked into saloons, singing hymns at the top of her lungs, and wrecked everything she saw with a hatchet.

Nation had been led to this dramatic course of action by the death of her first husband through alcoholism. Despite frequent arrests for disturbing the peace and destroying property, she never gave up her mission. Through her well-publicized crusade, Nation became a celebrity, toured the country ceaselessly, and was even invited to Europe to lecture on the evils of drink.

Temperance groups managed to get a number of laws passed. As of 1900, five states were already "dry." By 1910, eight

An editorial cartoon depicts the infamous temperance proponent Carry Nation, axe in hand. The caption reads, "I cannot tell a lie, I did it with my little hatchet."

states were dry and others had local areas where alcohol was illegal. The ultimate victory came later in the century: in 1919 the Eighteenth Amendment to the Constitution brought in the era of Prohibition, when the manufacture and sale of alcoholic beverages was completely outlawed in the United States.

Civil Rights

The situation for minority groups such as African Americans was bleak. De-

spite efforts by black leaders and their white colleagues, great strides in civil rights would not occur until later in the century.

About 80 percent of America's blacks still lived in only eleven southern states. About 200,000 of these people moved north between 1890–1910. The number was small when compared to the next decade, however, when upwards of a million black Americans would move in

Still Prejudiced

Times were bad for black men and women during the 1900s, especially so in the southern states. The number of lynchings was still high, the Ku Klux Klan was waging its campaign of terror, and segregation was a fact of life. When President Roosevelt invited the eminent black educator, Booker T. Washington, to eat at the White House, only a month after he took office in 1901, southern whites were outraged. As George Mowry reports in his book *The Era of Theodore Roosevelt*, the Memphis *Commercial-Appeal* newspaper fumed, "No Southern woman with proper self-

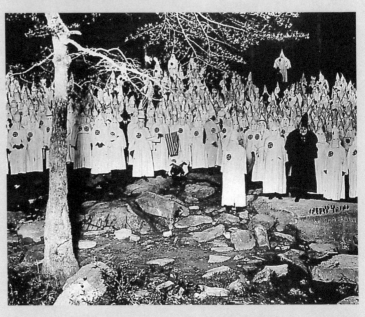

The Ku Klux Klan gathers in a nighttime raid. Anger at recent immigrants helped fuel Klan activities.

respect would now accept an invitation to the White House."

search of factory jobs and life in big cities.

Most African Americans were still locked in a cycle of poverty and ignorance that had prevailed since the end of the Civil War. Illiteracy among blacks was 45 percent in 1900, and was still high at 30 percent by 1910. Few schools admitted blacks, and many southern states had even effectively blocked black people from voting by passing voting laws requiring lit-

eracy. Though allegedly the civil rights of blacks were protected by federal laws, in practice these laws were flagrantly ignored by local governments.

Still, there were improvements. Booker T. Washington joined with other prominent African Americans and white progressive activists in a series of organizations that coalesced in 1910 with the formation of the National Association for the Advancement of Colored People (NAACP). This group would, in time, become one of the prime movers in the battle for civil rights.

Women's Rights

At the turn of the century, a quarter of the states in America denied a wife the right to own property, a third allowed her no claim on her earnings, and nearly all denied her equal share in the guardianship of her children. New York City passed a law forbidding women to smoke. Women in Kentucky could not legally make wills. Furthermore, only a handful of states allowed women's suffrage, that is, gave them the vote.

Nonetheless, during the 1900s women exercised an increasing amount of power in the reform movement. Historians William A. Link and Arthur S. Link assert, "It is no exaggeration to say

Members of a women's club proclaim their desire to promote women's rights. Many women reformers and activists were from the middle-to-upper classes.

that progressivism derived much of its vitality and impact from the participation of women."[26]

Most of the women involved in reform movements, including the women's rights movement, were middle- or upper-class women who had the time and resources to devote to their causes. Their participation often took the form of organized women's clubs. These groups grew dramatically during the decade; the membership of an umbrella organization, the General Federation of Women's Clubs, grew from fifty thousand in 1898 to over a million by 1914.

These clubs lobbied actively for the vote for women, although they would not get it nationwide until 1920. Meanwhile, women also worked in other ways to better the world outside their own homes. They performed many needed tasks, such as providing tutoring to recent immigrants, sewing clothes for needy families, and establishing libraries in areas neglected by the Carnegie library system. Hundreds of libraries across the country in schools, churches, stores, town halls, hospitals, prisons, asylums, and even lumber camps were established by women's clubs.

Even if they still considered themselves primarily homemakers, many female activists recognized that improving the world was a necessary adjunct to taking care of their own families. Inspired by famous women, such as political activists Mother Jones and Emma Goldman and pioneering birth-control advocate Margaret Sanger, many women began to realize that change in the world outside their own environments was long overdue. As activist Mary Beard put it, "Having learned that effectively to 'swat the fly' they must swat its nest, women have also learned that to swat disease they must swat poor housing, evil labor conditions, ignorance, and vicious interests."[27]

Civil rights, public health, the plight of immigrants, urban renewal, and political reform were only some of the issues improved during the 1900s. Teddy Roosevelt also led a charge against unfair businesses, and he brokered as well an uneasy truce between big business and the rising power of organized labor.

Chapter Three

The leader of an early labor union gives a speech to crowds of men that represent different workers' groups. The decade was marked by workers' efforts to obtain better working conditions and pay.

Big Business, Labor, and Trust Busting: An Era of Reform

Industrialization brought sweeping changes to American society, working conditions, and business. The rise of organized labor, the growth of big business, and the efforts of the federal government to intervene and control conflicts between the two were some of the most important events of the 1900s.

The changes created by industrialization took many forms. Huge numbers of workers were needed in factories and mills, in plants producing the new energy sources of electricity and oil, and in the nation's railroads and ports to transport materials cross-country.

Changes also occurred in the locations and ways people lived. They occurred as well in the way businessmen created companies, and in how business dealt with employees.

Workers had already begun organizing themselves into unions, which fought for the rights of their members. During the 1900s, the size and power of these unions increased dramatically. The differing needs and desires of the two groups, business and labor, were often so different that they led to strikes and other serious conflicts.

At the same time, business continued a growing trend toward consolidation. Most of the wealth and production were concentrated in a very few large companies. As a result, smaller companies were being squeezed out of business and fair competition was scarcer. Businesses often engaged in other unethical practices.

In the past, American government had done little to intervene in business affairs, either in negotiating between labor and management or in regulating business. This changed dramatically during the 1900s, however, as Theodore Roosevelt led a fight on two fronts. First, he instituted a policy in which government actively intervened between labor and business. Also, he

waged a campaign to regulate unethical business practices.

Government regulation of business is taken for granted today, but in the 1900s it was a radical concept. It fit in, however, with the general mood of reform that was sweeping the country. In his autobiography, Roosevelt reflected that he had used regulation and intervention to control "a riot of individualistic materialism, under which complete freedom for the individual . . . turned out in practice to mean perfect freedom for the strong to wrong the weak."[28]

Low Wages, Long Hours

For some workers, life was not bad. Certain immigrant groups, for example, found America far better than the countries they had left behind. Historians Oscar Theodore Barck Jr. and Nelson Manfred Blake note, "By comparison with Europe . . . the United States was a land of good wages and advantageous working conditions."[30]

Nonetheless, there was vast room for improvement. One major reason why workers were discontent concerned wages.

As of 1900, virtually no laws forced businesses to pay minimum wages or to guarantee that workers could keep their jobs. Plenty of workers could be found to replace anyone who got sick or caused trouble. Also, the flood of immigrants provided a vast pool of workers willing to labor for low wages. As a result, many owners of businesses and factories regarded workers only as commodities—as part of a big machine. They were something that could be purchased at the cheapest price and discarded whenever the owner wanted.

If business was good, workers might keep their jobs and perhaps be paid a little more. If business got bad, a worker's wages, which might already be barely enough to support a family, would be cut. If business got really bad, workers could be fired without notice or compensation. If a worker got sick or injured, he could also be fired and replaced immediately.

Along with the low pay went long hours. In 1900 the five-day week did not exist. People routinely worked six or even seven days a week, although some office workers had half-days on Saturday. The average work week was thus sixty hours, and seventy-hour weeks were not unusual.

Working Conditions

Another reason for dissatisfaction among workers was the condition of workplaces. As of 1900, no laws existed forcing business owners to provide even minimally decent job sites.

As a result, people often labored in factories and mills that were dark,

noisy, cold, and dirty. These often lacked proper rest rooms, safety precautions, and fire escapes. Agricultural workers, meanwhile, lived crammed together in tiny shacks without proper sanitary facilities.

Safety was also a major problem. Although some states had laws governing safety or providing compensation in case of an accident, these were rarely enforced. Furthermore, several decades would pass before federal laws were passed that regulated safety or compensated workers in case of injury.

Because of this, the accident rate was higher in U.S. factories, mines, and railroads than in any other industrial nation. According to a survey from 1907, half a million Americans annually were killed, crippled, or seriously injured while on the job. An average of twelve railroad men a week were killed. Mining was almost as dangerous; between 1900 and 1910, eighty-four explosions and cave-ins killed some twenty-five hundred men.

Poor working conditions also caused life-threatening illnesses, such as poisoning from phosphorus or lead production and black lung disease among miners. Even for those who did not work with chemicals or minerals, unhealthy working conditions often aggravated diseases such as tuberculosis.

Men work in a mine shaft deep underground. Conditions in the mines were notoriously dangerous—2,500 men died during the decade in mining accidents.

In rural areas, conditions were often dire. The air might be cleaner, but factors such as unsanitary conditions and poor nutrition were serious health hazards for the average farmworker.

Oscar Ameringer, an activist for workers' rights, toured Oklahoma farms in the 1900s, recording the lives of poor sharecropping farmers. He described young men, still under twenty, who were already toothless and severely weakened by hookworm and malnutrition: "[T]ottering old wrecks with the infants of their fourteen-year-old wives on their laps . . . I saw humanity at its lowest possible level of degradation and decay."[31]

Child Labor

The widespread use of child labor was another serious problem in the workplace. Most states had laws to protect children, but these usually applied only to children employed in factories and were often not enforced.

One survey in 1900 estimated that 10 percent of American girls between ten and fifteen years old, and 20 percent of boys the same age, had jobs. This meant that nearly two million children under the age of sixteen were employed in the country's factories, shops, and farms.

The estimated twenty-five thousand boys who worked in America's mines and quarries each received about sixty cents for a backbreaking ten-hour day. In canneries, boys and girls often cut fruits or vegetables for up to sixteen hours a day. In West Virginia, children as young as twelve could legally be put to work for any number of hours, day or night.

Conditions were especially bad in the cotton mills of the South, where an estimated twenty thousand young people worked. Children laboring at looms on the night shift in these factories were kept awake by having cold water periodically thrown in their faces. Horrifying accidents, such as the loss of a limb or even scalping if hair got caught

Mother Jones on the March

Some of the decade's most significant strikes focused on the plight of child laborers. One of the most famous began when seventy-five thousand Philadelphia textile workers walked off the job in 1903 demanding safer conditions. Ten thousand of these workers were children, many of them already mutilated or crippled by industrial accidents.

A legendary labor activist, Mother Jones, organized the children into an "army" that marched to visit Roosevelt. Along the way, they were met by farmers and others sympathetic to their cause, and these supporters supplied the marchers with food and shelter. Also along the way, Jones held press conferences at which she held forth with such fiery statements like this one reprinted in *America Enters the World*: "Philadelphia's mansions were built on the broken bones, the quivering hearts and drooping heads of these children."

Although Roosevelt refused to see the protesters, Jones ended the march with a huge rally in New York City that generated tremendous publicity. The Pennsylvania legislature was eventually pressured into prohibiting children under fourteen from taking part in factory work.

in machinery, were almost common-place.

Faced with these and other problems, employees increasingly began banding together in unions. These organized groups tried to force employers to improve conditions and wages, and they also lobbied to pass laws favoring workers.

Unions were originally organized by trade. Craftsmen with particular skills, such as carpentry or plumbing, banded together to set standard wages and prices for their services. As industrialization progressed and became more complex, however, unions sometimes represented all the various workers in a factory.

The back of a child miner is already bowed by the constant bending his job requires. Child labor was rampant—2 million children under the age of sixteen were employed.

Gompers, Debs, and Haywood

Almost universally, business owners and unions were in bitter opposition. The owners argued that only they had the right to make decisions about business practices. Many politicians and members of the public also saw unions as a threat to public safety, since they sometimes advocated disruptive or violent actions.

Bitter division often existed among workers about how to organize. No one group achieved complete control over the way labor

52

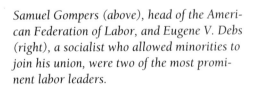

Samuel Gompers (above), head of the American Federation of Labor, and Eugene V. Debs (right), a socialist who allowed minorities to join his union, were two of the most prominent labor leaders.

organized itself. The era's three most important labor leaders, Samuel Gompers, Eugene Debs, and Bill Haywood, represented the main approaches to union organization.

Gompers was a burly man who headed the American Federation of Labor (AFL), an association of unions mostly representing skilled workers. By 1900, the AFL was the most influential force in organized labor. (In the 1950s, the AFL merged with a breakoff organization, the Committee for Industrial Organization, and became known as the AFL-CIO.)

The AFL was relatively conservative. Its unions concentrated on getting higher wages, shorter workdays, and better working conditions. Since member unions could set their own rules, women, blacks, and recent immigrant groups were often excluded from membership and thus from the higher paying jobs available through them.

The efforts of Eugene Debs were somewhat more radical. Debs was a socialist who believed that only political change and a complete economic reorganization could solve America's labor problems. Debs and his colleagues worked to organize unskilled workers, such as those in textile factories and railroads, and welcomed minorities excluded from the AFL.

Further to the political left was "Big Bill" Haywood, who led the Industrial Workers of the World (IWW). The Wobblies, as they were nicknamed, were a conglomerate of radical left-wing groups allied with both socialist and communist activists. Especially strong among laborers in the West, such as lumbermen, migratory workers, and miners, the Wobblies advocated violent, revolutionary action such as militant strikes and even bombings.

The Coal Strike

The primary way unions could force an issue was to walk off the job and go out on strike. Thousands of strikes occurred during the 1900s, organized by any of the several competing union groups. Most of these strikes were

Labor on Trial

The decade's most notorious labor trial stemmed from a murder. It came to represent the bitter divisions between organized union supporters and the business class.

As governor of Idaho, Frank Steunenberg had vehemently opposed attempts to unionize the state's mines. In December 1905, Steunenberg was killed in Caldwell, Idaho, when a booby-trapped gate exploded. An ex-union boss named T. S. Hogan was soon suspected.

Hogan, also known as Harry Orchard and Albert Horseley, was already wanted for a bombing in Colorado. He eventually confessed that he had rigged the Steunenberg bomb, acting on orders from the Western Federation of Miners. Union chief "Big Bill" Haywood and two others were arrested and put on trial, defended by the renowned labor lawyer, Clarence Darrow.

The trial was for many symbolic of the fight between capitalism and labor, and thousands marched in parades around the country in support of the defendants. Furthermore, while jailed in Idaho, Haywood ran for governor of Colorado on the Socialist ticket and received sixteen thousand votes. Though many felt he was guilty, Haywood and his co-defendants were eventually acquitted due to a lack of evidence.

William H. Haywood, leader of the Industrial Workers of the World, an organization of several radical left-wing groups.

Mine Workers walked off their jobs in the coal fields in Pennsylvania. This strike was important mainly because it was the first in which the federal government played a significant role.

The strike affected nearly everyone in America, since coal was still an extremely important fuel. As winter approached, people feared that homes, offices, schools, and hospitals across the country might be without heat. The public and press strongly urged a quick end to the problem.

Roosevelt stepped in to arbitrate—that is, act as a referee—between the feuding parties by inviting them to hold talks at the White House. The president was impressed with the integrity of the workers' representatives, but he was appalled at what he called the "arrogant stupidity" of the mine owners.

Typical of this arrogance was a patronizing comment by mine owner George F. Baer. Baer commented publicly that laborers should not worry, because they would be taken care of "by the Christian men to whom God, in his infinite wisdom, has given control of the property interests of the country."[31]

Settling the Dispute

When the mine owners and workers could not reach a compromise, Roosevelt threatened to send ten thousand

relatively small and short-lived, and were resolved peacefully. However, some were bitter and protracted, and some were marked by violence.

One of the decade's most significant strikes began in the fall of 1902, when fifty thousand members of the United army troops to operate the mines. However, before that became necessary he negotiated an agreement. The miners received most of their demands, including a 10 percent wage raise and shorter hours. It was a victory for the workers and a major turning point in government relations toward labor disputes.

Many strikes were marked by violence. In 1910, a dispute between labor and antiunion forces in Los Angeles led to a bomb explosion at the *Los Angeles Times* building that killed twenty people. Also in 1910, sixty thousand garment workers in New York City, many of them women, struck for better conditions. Thugs hired by business owners taunted and attacked protesters on picket lines. Widely reported stories of young women being harassed and beaten had a powerful effect on public sympathy.

President Theodore Roosevelt sits with adviser Elihu Root and financier J. Pierpont Morgan in their efforts to solve the coal strike of 1902. Roosevelt's involvement marked the first time that the federal government helped negotiate labor disputes.

Too Many Strikes

"Mr. Dooley" was a fictional Irish bartender who discussed current affairs in a popular humorous newspaper column by Finley Peter Dunne. This excerpt from a 1906 column (reprinted in *The Progressive Years*) makes fun of labor unions.

Somebody is sthrikin' all th' time. Wan day th' horseshoers are out, an' another day th' teamsters. Th' Brotherhood iv Molasses Candy Pullers sthrikes, an' th' Amalgymated Union iv Pickle Sorters quits in sympathy. Th' carpinter that has been puttin' up a chicken coop f'r Hogan knocked off wurruk whin he found that Hogan was shavin' himsilf without a card fr'm th' Barbers' Union. Hogan fixed it with th' walkin' dillygate iv th' barbers, an' th' carpinter quit wurruk because he found that Hogan was wearin' a pair iv non-union pants. Hogan wint down-town an' had his pants unionized an' come home to find that th' carpinter had sthruck because Hogan's hens was layin' eggs without th' union label.

Roosevelt was generally sympathetic toward labor, although he denounced the radicalism and violence of some union leaders. Roosevelt's efforts to find a middle ground between the excesses of owners and the radicalism of union agitators marked the beginning of what has become a long-standing policy making government an important element in resolving issues between workers and business. According to historian George E. Mowry, by the end of the Roosevelt era "[t]he government . . . had become a third force and partner in major labor disputes."[32]

Regulating Big Business

Until the 1900s, government had generally let businesses, especially large corporations, have their own way. Roosevelt and his Progressivist colleagues dramatically changed this, enacting regulations controlling many aspects of business.

He was especially concerned with problems involving very large corporations called trusts. A trust was an organization that combined several related firms, creating a monopoly on a particular commodity.

For example, a trust might own mines from which raw ore could be produced, railroads to transport the ore, smelting operations to turn the ore into a usable metal such as steel, and factories to create finished products out of the steel. By controlling a product in such a way, a trust could set its own prices, because there was little or no competition in the various stages of the operation.

Roosevelt realized that trusts, and business in general, played an important role in America's rise to prosperity.

However, he also believed that many aspects of commerce were out of control. He did not want to destroy big business; he simply wanted it to be more responsible.

This attitude became clear almost immediately after he took office. In his first annual message to Congress, in December 1901, Roosevelt declared:

> Captains of industry . . . have on the whole done great good to our people. Without them the material development of which we are so justly proud could never have taken place. . . . Yet it is also true that there are real and grave evils.[33]

Trusts

The rise of trusts was swift during the 1900s. Only twelve major trusts were formed between 1879 and 1897, and in 1899 alone some 185 trusts were formed. By 1904, however, 305 trusts controlled nearly half of the country's total manufacturing capital—a small number of companies to have such a large amount of power.

The steel business is an example of how trusts could quickly dominate an industry. America more than doubled the amount of steel it produced between 1900 and 1910, although the number of companies making it dropped dramatically. In 1880 over a thousand steel-manufacturing compa-

nies existed in America, but by 1900 only seventy remained. In 1901, when Andrew Carnegie consolidated many of these companies into the largest single trust of the era, U.S. Steel, the competition dropped to almost nothing.

The stories were similar in other industries. Six railroad trusts controlled 95 percent of the nation's tracks. J. D. Rockefeller's Standard Oil controlled about 85 percent of the domestic oil industry. Industries ranging from life insurance and finance to meatpacking experienced the same situation, in which a few companies held virtual monopolies. By 1903, 40 percent of America's output was produced by only 1 percent of the companies in the country.

Trust-Busting Begins

Defenders of trusts argued that they lowered prices for consumers by standardizing practices and producing in mass quantities. Those who opposed them argued that trusts destroyed fair competition by eliminating traditional, independently owned small businesses.

A law meant to control monopolies, the Sherman Anti-Trust Act, had existed since the 1890s. However, it had never been effectively enforced. Shortly after he took office, Roosevelt instructed his attorney general, Philander Knox, to

Banker J. P. Morgan was part of the Northern Securities trust that included two railroad magnates. Morgan's trust would be the first that Roosevelt would attempt to break up.

begin using the Sherman Act against his first target, Northern Securities.

Northern Securities was a huge railroad monopoly that allied three of America's most powerful tycoons: banker J. P. Morgan and railroaders E. H. Harriman and James J. Hill. Attacking these three first, Roosevelt knew, would strike at the very center of American business.

The news of Roosevelt's assault on the powerful company sent a shock wave through the business community, and the three Northern Securities leaders were outraged. Accompanied by two sympathetic senators, Morgan hurried to the White House to confront Roosevelt. Thinking that the issue was simply a problem between two rival business concerns, Morgan arrogantly declared, "If we have done anything wrong, send your man to my man and they can fix it up." [34]

The struggle to dissolve Northern Securities continued for several years, and in the end Roosevelt was victorious. In 1904 the Supreme Court ordered the trust dissolved.

The message sent to big business and the public was that Roosevelt was serious about trust-busting, and that the government could effectively control large corporations. As Roosevelt put it, "I favored them while they did right and was not in the least afraid of them when they did wrong."[35]

Such actions were extremely popular with the general public and the press. They generally rejoiced that big business was no longer an unstoppable force. One journal noted at the time, "Even Morgan no longer rules the earth, and other men may still do business without asking his permission."[36]

Teddy Roosevelt wields his "big stick" in his trust-busting efforts. Roosevelt is still tied to this big-stick image.

Further Acts

While the Northern Securities case was pending, Congress passed other antitrust laws and pursued other antitrust cases. Successful trust-busting suits were brought against offenders in such major industries as meat, oil, and tobacco. In all, Roosevelt initiated forty-four antitrust suits, and his successor, William Howard Taft, began ninety.

Roosevelt also established or expanded a number of official agencies to address specific problems and administer laws regarding commerce. One important agency he strengthened was the Interstate Commerce Commission (ICC). The ICC had existed since 1887, but it had been relatively ineffective. During the 1900s, a number of laws increased its power and scope. Chief among these were the 1905 Hepburn Act, which gave the ICC greater power to regulate railroads, and the 1910 Mann-Elkins Act, which extended its power over phone, telegraph, and cable concerns.

Roosevelt also acknowledged the importance of business and unions to the nation's well-being when he established, in 1903, a cabinet-level Department of Commerce and Labor. In 1913, this office was divided into separate departments governing commerce and labor.

As Roosevelt was pursuing his trust-busting, several states passed legislation of their own. The Missouri legislature, for example, banned Standard Oil from operating within its borders.

Progressive reform measures on a national scale were not limited to labor and business. Important steps were also taken throughout the 1900s in the areas of wilderness conservation and the settlement of rural areas.

Chapter Four

Theodore Roosevelt poses with naturalist John Muir on Glacier Point above Yosemite Valley, California. Roosevelt put the power of the federal government behind setting aside land for the public's use.

Saving the Wilderness and Settling the Land

Progressive reformers in the 1900s were concerned not only with improving cities, government organizations, and the lives of people. Some of the decade's most sweeping and long-lasting reforms were directed at the land itself.

Many of these efforts were enacted on a national scale. In some cases, it meant a fight to control the development of resources or to preserve pristine wilderness for future generations. In other cases, it was an effort to improve existing farmland. Still other cases involved homesteading and bringing water to the arid, underpopulated lands of the western states.

The United States has always been

rich in resources. Only in this century, however, has there been an organized effort to preserve those resources.

In its first century, America paid little attention to environmental concerns. Minerals, water, and timber were abundantly available to early settlers.

Up through the time of industrialization, few people seriously thought that the nation's resources might someday be exhausted, or worried that its air and water could be permanently damaged. As a result, factories belched smoke and dumped waste, miners stripped huge expanses of land, and loggers clear-cut indiscriminately. Often, resources were so abundant that vast amounts of material were wasted. Loggers who cut down the giant sequoias of California often left behind most of each tree as trash. Miners were often nearly as wasteful when they extracted ore from the ground.

Slowly, however, attitudes about the unregulated use of natural resources began to shift. By the turn of the century, the destruction was becoming so great that many people were beginning to worry. At the same time, a related movement was growing, concerned with preserving still-untouched wilderness land. This was

Naturalist John Muir founded the Sierra Club and worked to educate the public about the need to set aside land for future generations to enjoy.

the beginning of what is now called the conservation movement. Through the efforts of early conservationists like John Muir, founder of the Sierra Club, Americans were becoming aware of their natural environment to an unprecedented degree.

Balancing Interests

When Roosevelt became president in 1901, conservationists like Muir gained an important ally. Roosevelt was a lifelong champion of the outdoors. A tireless hiker and camper and an avid hunter, Roosevelt had a great respect for the beauty of wilderness and a deep desire to see it preserved.

At the same time, he was a practical-minded politician who realized that development was inevitable to a degree. In particular, he was eager to see the undeveloped prairie land of the Midwest and West become fertile and prosperous. One of his main accomplishments as president was to enact legislation that balanced the desires of conservationists with those of city planners and others who required the use of natural resources.

These various groups of politicians, businessmen, and members of the public had widely divergent ideas about how to handle issues regarding the land. Easterners, for instance, were generally not urgently in need of developing natural resources. They were more concerned with preserving wilderness areas, without development, for aesthetic and recreational reasons—that is, for the sheer enjoyment of the beauty of the wilderness. They therefore generally supported the government's conservation work.

The situation was different in the West. Many westerners who otherwise supported Roosevelt did their best to

Birth of the Teddy Bear

A 1902 issue of the *Washington Star* featured a cartoon by Clifford Berryman captioned: "Drawing the Line in Mississippi." It showed Teddy Roosevelt, rifle in hand, with his back turned to a cowering bear cub.

The reference was to a hunting expedition Roosevelt had recently undertaken in Mississippi. His hosts, wishing the president to return home with a suitable trophy, had trapped a bear cub for him to shoot. However, Roosevelt refused to fire at the helpless creature.

Berryman's cartoon received nationwide publicity. A Russian immigrant toy manufacturer in New York, Morris Michtom, made a stuffed bear cub toy with button eyes and put it in his shop window along with the cartoon. Soon, dozens of eager customers were in his shop, requesting their own "Teddy's bears" (as they were originally called).

The toy was so popular that the following year Michtom formed a company exclusively to manufacture them. Their popularity spread quickly, and soon teddy bears, in many varieties and often sporting their own custom-made clothes and hats, became the most popular toys of their day.

block his conservation efforts. Instead, they favored the rapid development of resources.

For instance, since the forests of the Midwest were already more or less logged out, western lumbermen were eager to exploit the vast forests of the Pacific Northwest and northern California. The building of dams was also generally supported in the West. This was especially so in urban areas like San Francisco, where water was needed, and in the Southwest, where irrigation for ranching depended on dams and the reclamation of desert lands.

Pinchot

Roosevelt's chief ally in studying issues concerning natural resources was Gifford Pinchot, the nation's leading authority on forestry. Beginning during the McKinley administration and hitting his stride under Roosevelt, Pinchot completely restructured and revitalized the federal forestry system. He greatly expanded the government's forestry program, brought several scattered agencies together into one streamlined operation, and guided the cohesive new Forest Service through its formative years.

Like Roosevelt, Pinchot had a practical frame of mind that accepted controlled development or use of federally

Gifford Pinchot, head of the federal government's fledgling Forest Service, tried to strike a compromise between developers and conservationists.

owned resources as necessary. The forester passionately believed that federal land should serve "the greatest number." By this, he meant that the nation's resources should benefit the largest percentage possible of the general public, not a handful of developers looking for profit or a handful of conservationists wanting to preserve it untouched.

In general, he believed, resources should be conserved whenever possible. However, there had to be some compromise. People needed wood for houses, for instance; therefore, a certain amount of carefully logged forest land was allowable if the land was also reseeded and maintained. People needed electricity; controlled development of dams and hydroelectric stations, therefore, was also acceptable. In a 1905 statement known as the "Pinchot Letter," he summarized his philosophy as a belief in "the greatest good, for the greatest number [of people], for the longest time." [37]

Conservationists vs. Developers

One of the bitterest battles in the 1900s between conservationists and developers concerned efforts to dam the scenic

The Hetch Hetchy Dam was supposed to provide San Francisco with a new water supply. Instead, it was a fiasco, flooding beautiful wilderness for little concrete benefit.

Hetch Hetchy Valley near Yosemite Park in California.

The conflict began as a regional debate. The city of San Francisco wanted the water and electricity the project promised. Local conservationists like John Muir warned that damming the valley would not only destroy precious wilderness but would fail to provide the promised rewards.

Congress and the president became embroiled in the controversy. Roosevelt tried to remain neutral, hoping to placate both sides, but eventually decided that developing the valley was more important than preserving it. In 1913, a dam was finally approved by Congress.

Muir's prediction that the development would not live up to expectations was correct. Partly out of embarrassment over this affair, Congress later approved laws that expanded and strengthened the national park system. A local controversy thus had wideranging implications in what would eventually be called the environmental movement. Writer Edward Weinstock notes, "For the first time in American history, the conflict between preservation and civilization was fought on a national scale." [38]

Monuments

During Roosevelt's administration, millions of acres were added to existing national forest and park lands. Nearly 150 million acres, about three-quarters of the land in today's national forest system, were set aside during the 1900s.

Roosevelt also protected several areas with especially unusual features by proclaiming them national monuments. The first was Devil's Tower in Wyoming, declared a monument in 1906. The same year, the Petrified Forest in Arizona also became a protected property. Other sites named as monuments during the Roosevelt administration included Natural Bridges in Utah (1908) and the Grand Canyon (1908). By 1910, twenty-three national monuments had been set aside.

Roosevelt also passed legislation protecting sites that were of archaeological or historical value. The most important of these laws was the Lacey Antiquities Act of 1906, the first federal law of its kind. It protected a variety of locations, from mining ghost towns to Native American burial grounds. Furthermore, Roosevelt was the first president to create national wildlife refuges, which guaranteed protection for endangered birds, animals, and plant life. The first of these was Pelican Island in Florida, established in 1903.

A number of important governing bodies were established during the 1900s to oversee the regulation of

Sightseers visit the southern rim of the Grand Canyon in the early 1900s. The automobile helped make visiting the newly opened national parks a reality for many Americans.

Natural Resources. Many pieces of legislation regulating the use of land not owned by the government were also passed. For instance, restrictions were placed on such destructive projects as coal mines, phosphate beds, and water-power sites.

Roosevelt often remarked later that, of all his accomplishments as president, he was most proud of his work to conserve wilderness. In 1947, Theodore Roosevelt National Memorial Park in North Dakota was established in honor of these achievements. Historian George Mowry adds that Roosevelt's efforts had a deep and lasting impact, and remain "among his most impressive and enduring achievements."[39]

Settling the Land

various aspects of land and natural resources. One of these was the National Commission for the Conservation of

The American frontier had officially closed by the turn of the century, but there were still huge tracts of land in the West that remained undeveloped, barren, and virtually population free. At the same time that the Roosevelt administration promoted the preservation and controlled use of wilderness and forest land, it also energetically backed the homesteading of these unsettled regions.

Roosevelt and his colleagues envisioned a vast, well-planned settlement that would bring prosperity to those who settled there. The chairman of the Rural Settlement Section of the National Irrigation Congress, a group of concerned experts, noted in 1905 that the nation had an

opportunity to start rural life on a plane never before known . . . by bringing settlers together into communities with social advantages, proper sanitation conditions, and better educational facilities than have ever been known outside the cities.[40]

Of particular interest was the settlement of areas that lacked sufficient irrigation. These regions did not attract commercial developers, since buying up dry land was a risky investment and

A family poses in front of the rural cabin they were able to build due to Roosevelt's Expanded Homestead Act. Roosevelt's desire to see the West more populated drove several pieces of legislation that made settling remote lands more appealing.

irrigating it was extremely expensive. Large-scale, government-sponsored development of electric power, irrigation plans, grazing programs, and other projects were needed to attract farmers and ranchers to these lands.

From the government's point of view, settling the dry West had several benefits. It would relieve pressure on overcrowded cities and increase the amount of land available to grow wheat and raise cattle for an eager market. It would, coincidentally, finance the completion of a transcontinental railroad network, as settlers moved west with their belongings and shipped produce and livestock back east. Writer Jonathan Raban notes, "Homesteading was the win-win-win solution to a whole raft of problems. . . . The homesteaders got their land, the corporations got their railroads, the cities lost their slums, and America had more food on the table."[41]

Aiding the Settlement

Several laws were passed during Roosevelt's tenure that aided in the development and settling of the West. One of the most important was the Newlands Reclamation Act of 1902, named for the Arizona senator who proposed it. This act stipulated that all money from the sale of government-owned lands be used to undertake irrigation projects that were too large for private or state resources.

By 1915, the federal government had invested $80 million, an enormous sum for the time, in twenty-five electrical and water projects. The largest of these was Roosevelt Dam in Arizona.

These projects were followed in succeeding decades by many others, including several massive ones undertaken by a future President Roosevelt, Theodore's distant relative, Franklin. Many of the large-scale irrigation projects that still provide water to the dry regions of the West today had their origins in the Newlands Reclamation Act.

A related and equally crucial law was passed in 1909. The Expanded Homestead Act enlarged and strengthened an existing law that allowed settlers to claim large tracts of land in sparsely populated areas. If settlers could "prove"—that is, cultivate and improve—a claim of land within a certain number of years, the land, called a homestead, legally became theirs.

The 1909 homestead law increased the size of an individual homestead to 320 acres, with the requirement that at least one quarter of the land be cultivated. If this was accomplished, the land title reverted to the homesteader after five years.

Author Charles F. Wilkinson writes, "Homestead entries boomed as new waves of settlers moved west to capitalize on the offer of nearly free farmland and water."[42] However, the promise of prosperity was more difficult to achieve than many first believed. The hardships of life on the prairie and the desert proved to be too much for thousands of would-be farmers and ranchers. Nonetheless, despite these frequent failures to make homesteads prosper, other recent arrivals in the dry West, often immigrants, were able to make the land bloom and grow.

Farmers

The years 1900–1910 were generally good ones for agriculture, for newcomers in the West, but even more so for farmers in established farming regions. The decade was part of a so-called Golden Age of agriculture that stretched from the turn of the century to 1920.

During this period, farm prices rose an astonishing 72 percent. The amount of cultivated land, overall productivity, and the value of farmland also rose during the decade. By 1910 the total value of all farm property was about $40 billion, twice that of the 1900 figure.

Much of this prosperity was due to the introduction of new methods of farming and of technological innovations. One of the most important of

Permanent Greatness and the Farmer Class

Teddy Roosevelt's 1908 letter appointing the Country Life Commission, a federal panel that studied the problems of settlement in the West, acknowledged both the greatness and the restrictions of the agricultural life. This excerpt is from *The Progressive Years.*

No nation has ever achieved permanent greatness unless this greatness was based on the well-being of the great farmer class, the men who live on the soil. . . . We Americans are making great progress in the development of our agricultural resources. But it is equally true that the social and economic institutions of the open country are not keeping pace with the development of the nation as a whole. The farmer is, as a rule, better off than his forbears; but his increase in well-being has not kept pace with that of the country as a whole.

these innovations was the perfection of the tractor. As of 1900, horses were still the most common form of farm power. As the decade progressed, however, vastly more efficient tractors, first steam powered and then gas powered, became more and more common.

There were only about 5,000 steam tractors in use on American farms in 1900. By 1910, that number had skyrocketed to 100,000. The number of gas tractors likewise rose, from a handful in

A farmer uses a steam plow and roller to farm on a large scale in South Dakota. Technological inventions such as the steam tractor significantly increased the productivity of America's farmers.

1900 to nearly 100,000 by 1910. Gradually, gas-powered tractors became dominant and the steam tractor was eventually abandoned. Frederick Lewis Allen writes, "The mechanization of the American farm [was] getting under way fast."[43]

Changes

Not everything during the 1900s was positive for American farmers, however. At the same time that they were experiencing unheard-of prosperity, powerful forces were already at work that would eventually alter the farmers' traditional ways of life.

Industry was becoming more and more dominant as an economic force in America. Within a few decades the nation's cities and towns would replace farm communities as centers of opportunity and political and cultural leadership.

Meanwhile, there was a shift away from the traditional small farm—that is, away from farmers who grew several crops, producing enough to feed their families plus, perhaps, a little surplus for their immediate neighbors. The trend instead, especially in the newly irrigated West, was toward the formation of large commercial farms and ranches. On these facilities, one commodity, such as wheat or cattle, was raised to send to far-off markets.

In 1800, nine out of ten Americans in the workforce lived on farms; by 1900, that figure had dropped to only one in three, and the downward trend continued throughout the decade and beyond. American agriculture would never recover its once-dominant position in the nation's economy and importance.

The conflicts between farming's prosperous present and its doubtful future were already being seen in the 1900s by American farmers and agriculture experts. These frictions were expressed in a paper written by the Country Life Commission, a group of experts appointed by Roosevelt to study the problem. In its report to the Senate in 1909, the committee wrote:

> There has never been a time when the American farmer was as well off as he is to-day, when we consider not only his earning power, but the comforts and advantages he may secure. Yet the real efficiency in farm life [must be measured] in terms of its possibilities. Considered from this point of view, there are very marked deficiencies.[44]

The shift away from agriculture as America's dominant force was quickened by many factors. Some of the most dramatic of these were the changes taking place in transportation, especially in the rise of a strange new machine called an automobile.

Chapter Five

An entire family gears up in their early roadsters to participate in a driving tour in 1910. The automobile allowed for greater travel and expanded horizons for many Americans.

Transportation Transformed: The Automobile Age Begins

At the beginning of the 1900s, communities were separated from one another to a degree that is hard to imagine today. Telephones were scarce; radios and other forms of mass communication did not exist, and even the postal service was unreli-

able in remote areas.

For local transportation, people used their feet or a horse and wagon. For a farmer who lived five miles outside the nearest town, hitching up the wagon and taking the family into town for church or an afternoon's shopping was a genuine event. Visiting friends who lived ten miles away was an all-day expedition because horses needed time to rest and be fed.

People who lived in the cities were also constrained in how far they could travel. Urbanites could take horse-drawn trolleys to distant parts of their cities, but often a city dweller's entire world was the immediate neighborhood.

The railroad, meanwhile, was the only option for long distances, and it was usually a dusty and time-consuming affair. Even for those with the time and money to travel to other countries, such as sailing to Europe, journeys were still time-consuming and often uncomfortable and dangerous. More often than not, therefore, Americans lived almost their entire lives among familiar people and familiar surroundings.

On the other hand, Americans have always been noted for their restlessness and ability to relocate. Historians Dorothy and Carl Schneider write, "No matter when they arrived in the United States, Americans have always moved around a lot."[45]

This tendency toward movement dramatically increased in the 1900s. Several factors went into this change. Though travel by airplane would not become common for decades, Orville and Wilbur Wright took an important step toward making it a reality with their successful 1903 flight. The rise of electrical trolleys and subways changed the way people traveled within cities. Most of all, the arrival of the automobile signaled a radical shift in the travel habits of Americans—and in the very landscape of the nation.

Railroads

For long-distance travel, and for transporting goods across vast expanses, the railroad was king.

By the end of the Civil War, 35,000 miles of railroad track had been laid in America. By 1900 that figure had ballooned to 198,000 miles of track criss-crossing the country. The American rail system was the largest and most efficiently managed system of its kind in the world. It was also one of the biggest business enterprises of the time. Rail expansion continued to increase rapidly until 1916, when it reached an all-time high of 254,000 miles of track.

The companies that controlled the railroads were also major real-estate developers, especially in the sparsely populated West. The railroads thus had an interest in getting people to settle along the routes where they owned land, and they became important elements in the West's expansion and settlement.

Existing cities vied fiercely to be included on new lines, and such

A construction crew poses before a wood-burning locomotive in the Cascade Mountains. The building of the railroad linked remote cities together, helping to join Americans into a single nation.

inclusion often spelled the difference between becoming prosperous or becoming a ghost town. As the lines were built, meanwhile, new towns grew up roughly forty miles apart, because that was how far trains could go before they needed to stop and replenish their supplies of water and coal.

The railroad industry played an important part in America's gradual shift from a loose collection of differing regions to a single nation bound closely together. Because they were so closely linked to the country's prosperity, railroads also were an important element in America's emergence as a major world power in the 1900s. Historians William A. Link and Arthur S. Link note, "It is impossible to comprehend the origins of the twentieth-century American economy without understanding the central importance of railroads."[46]

Trolleys and Subways

The railroads dominated long-distance travel, but for short-term travel within cities electric trolleys and subways were taking over from horse-drawn trolleys.

The change had begun before the turn of the century. In 1890, 78 percent of the nation's trolleys were horse-drawn; by 1900, that figure had dropped to only 2 percent. This trend continued, and by 1902 virtually all of the nation's streetcars were electric. This meant that only some three hundred miles of trolley routes were covered by horse trolleys, compared with twenty thousand miles covered by electric ones.

Chicago had the most extensive of these "electric traction" systems, with about a thousand miles of track. Some

of these systems were noisy, uncomfortable, and graceless. Many, however, were extremely elegant, with cultivated touches such as wicker chairs and brocade curtains. Others were exciting to ride, such as the cable cars that clattered over San Francisco's famous hills.

Subways also began to emerge during the 1900s as important means of urban transportation. Before the turn of the century, Boston had built a short subway line using regular trolley cars. The first real subway, however, was in New York, built after an unsuccessful attempt at creating elevated railways. Begun in 1900 and completed in 1904,

Subway kiosks mark an entrance and exit to New York's extensive subway system, begun in the early 1900s.

New York's subway ran almost the length of Manhattan, from the Brooklyn Bridge to 145th Street, and was soon expanded to include New York's other boroughs.

Air Traffic

People had dreamed about flying for thousands of years, and there had been countless unsuccessful experiments. Not until the 1900s, however, would anyone succeed in piloting a heavier-than-air craft.

Many believed such a feat was impossible. In 1903, the distinguished astronomer Simon Newcomb stated, "Aerial flight is one of that class of problems with which man can never cope." [47] Later that same year, two brothers proved him wrong.

Orville and Wilbur Wright owned a modest bicycle shop in Dayton, Ohio. For years, they had been tinkering with what they called a "whopper flying machine." In December 1903, using the sands of Kitty Hawk, North Carolina, as a testing ground, they succeeded in flying their flimsy craft on a series of wobbly flights, the longest lasting fifty-nine seconds and covering 852 feet. It was the world's first successful flight of a heavier-than-air craft.

Orville and Wilbur Wright attempt their historic flight in Kitty Hawk, North Carolina. Although the Wrights' flight would mark the beginning of a revolution in transportation, few people took notice of the historic moment.

Incredibly, no one took much notice. The day after the flight, only a handful of newspapers across the country thought the story was worth reporting. The Wrights were seen as just two more tinkerers fooling with flimsy gadgets.

When the efforts of the Wrights and other pioneer aerialists were noticed, they were generally seen as recreational rather than practical. No one guessed that airplanes might become anything more than a hobbyists' toy. When the *New York Times* got around to reporting on the Wrights' first flight, it did so on the sports page.

No special attention was paid Wilbur and Orville until 1908. That year, they demonstrated an improved version of their airplane to government officials. The following year, the Wrights received a contract to develop an airplane for the army. Of this slow acknowledgment of the Wrights' achievement, Frederick Lewis Allen writes, "The seed of the great aviation industry had been sown in 1903; it began to sprout, very belatedly, in 1908."[48]

In 1910 a popular song, "Come, Josephine, in My Flying Machine," paid homage to the new invention. However, flying did not experience a significant burst of growth until the next

No Commercial Future

Orville and Wilbur Wright's historic flight drew almost no attention from the nation's press in 1903. One editor, Keville Glennan of the Norfolk, Virginia, *Virginian-Pilot,* grasped its significance. Despite the Wrights' efforts to keep their triumph secret, Glennan learned about it through a leak in the local telegraph office when the Wrights cabled home. He bannered the news across his front page, but could not interest other editors in the story.

For years, most people thought flying machines were nothing more than crazy fads. Even the most enthusiastic fans thought of them as little more than exotic sporting equipment. As late as 1907, according to Walter Lord in *The Good Years*, a speaker at the International Aeronautical Congress stated that airplanes had no commercial or military future and that, at best, they might someday prove "useful in explorations of otherwise inaccessible places, such as mountain tops, swamps, or densely wooded regions." In 1911, aviation expert W. B. Kaempffert stated his belief that the invention would probably remain "a racing machine for gilded youth."

decade, when the need for military craft for World War I spurred development. It was not until 1914, moreover, that the first passenger airline was established.

The Auto Age Begins

Without a doubt, the most important development in transportation during the 1900s was the rise of the gas-powered automobile. This rise was swift: in 1900 the car industry did not exist, but by 1914 it was the eighth-largest industry in the country. Cars had an enormous effect on the economy of the nation, on the lives of individual citizens and society in general, and on the very shape of the landscape.

In the years since, cars have affected everything from the growth of cities to vacation patterns, business and shopping practices, and sharp rises in pollution and accident statistics. Their dependence on oil-based fuel and their need for regularly repaved and ever-lengthening roadways, meanwhile, have significantly affected the shape of

A man drives a 1902 gas-driven Oldsmobile, which averaged a speed of fourteen miles per hour.

American industry. Overall, Page Smith notes, cars ultimately became powerful symbols of America itself:

Americans could escape from the stultifying details of daily life to a realm of speed and fantasy [with cars]. . . . The automobile changed radically the relationship of human beings to the physical world, to nature, to one another. It became a courtship machine, a mobile love nest (with the invention of that splendid space the rumble seat), a symbol of success, of America. . . . The engine itself became the god of youth. Mysterious to their elders, it yielded up all its mysteries to its young devotees. It represented, perhaps above all, the conquest of the vast space that constituted America.[49]

"Get a Horse!"

"Horseless carriages" in various configurations had been around since well before the turn of the century. A number of people in the United States and Europe deserve at least part of the credit for their invention.

The number of cars in America was small at the turn of the century. In 1895, there were only four cars on America's highways. By 1900, only four thousand autos were being produced yearly in America. They were so rare that it had been estimated that only half the population had ever even seen one.

The earliest cars were not very practical, and there were few reasons to have one beyond sheer novelty. They were essentially playthings for the mechanically minded, the adventurous, and the rich.

One reason is that cars were expensive. Also, they required constant care. Their frequent breakdowns (and the lack of garages except in the biggest cities) required that all drivers be mechanics, or, at least, bring mechanics with them. Cars were so cumbersome and unreliable that the sarcastic cry "Get a horse!" became a term of scorn toward any hapless driver struggling with a balky machine.

Few comforts existed for drivers on the road. There were almost no paved highways outside towns; anyone who wanted to drive a car had to be prepared to deal with dirt roads and their attendant mud, dust, deep ruts, and potholes. There were also no filling stations. The first gas station would not appear until 1907; until then, drivers bought gas at general stores in five-gallon cans.

The rich often used their cars as sports equipment. They made a game of speeding, racing down city streets at a breathtaking fifteen or eighteen miles

Garages on Wheels

Driving a car in the 1900s was nothing if not adventurous. Motorists had to be well prepared to double as mechanics in the face of poor roads, frequent breakdowns, and infrequent garages. A typical set of motorist's supplies, adapted from a list in Time-Life's book *1900–1910*, might include the following:

TOOLS

Tire chains
Jack
Brace wrench for changing rims
Tire pump
Tire gauge
Valve tool
Small vulcanizer
Fine sandpaper
Fine emery cloth
Special wrenches belonging to car
Monkey wrenches
Small set of socket wrenches
Small Stillson wrench
Screwdrivers
Pair pliers with wire cutters
Jackknife
Small vise to clamp to running board
Machinist's hammer
Punch or carpenter's nail set
Cotter-pin extractor
Large flat mill file
Thin knife-edged file
Small short-handled axe
Towing cable
Oil can
Grease gun
Funnel
Chamois skin

Pocket electric flashlight
Pocket ammeter (an instrument for measuring current)

SPARE PARTS

Extra tire casings and inner tubes
Two-gallon can of gasoline
Two-quart can of engine oil
Can of grease
Can of kerosene
Blowout patch
Leather tire sleeve
Package of assorted cement patches
Small package of raw rubber for vulcanizing
Small can of vulcanizing cement
Tube of self-vulcanizing cement
Can of mastic
Extra tire valves
Extra valve caps
Extra dust caps
Extra headlight bulbs
Extra taillight bulbs
Insulated wire
Electrician's tape
Extra spark plugs
Extra porcelains for cylinders
Ball of asbestos wicking
Bundle waste
Assortment gaskets to fit car
Piece of radiator steam hose
Extra hose clips
Extra valve springs
Extra fan belt
Rubber packing
Assortment of cotter pins, nuts, lock washers, wood screws, and nails

an hour—much faster than the typical ten-miles-an-hour speed limit. Policemen would vainly chase the offenders and try to catch them on bicycles.

At first, well-to-do automobilists rebelled at the idea of regulations governing their new pastime. The duke of Manchester, visiting New York with his American bride, was indignant when he discovered that he could not have a driver's license simply for the asking. "A duke who is fit to be trusted with an American wife," he huffed, "is certainly fit to be trusted with a 'bubble' in New York, provided he knows how to run it." [50]

Gradual Improvements

No one was even sure what to call the new machines. Among the early terms for the new "horseless carriages" were motocycle, petrocar, viamote, mocle, and mobe (pronounced mo-bee). Wealthy people often referred to their shiny metal toys as bubbles.

No one seemed to know what laws to pass to control the new beasts. In 1902 Vermont passed a law stating that all cars had to have adults running in front of them carrying red warning flags. In Tennessee, drivers were required to post a week's notice before starting on a trip.

With a constant barrage of technical improvements, however, autos gradually became safer, more reliable, and more commonplace. Among these improvements were better tires, a steering wheel that replaced the original tiller-like control, and an electric starter that eliminated the need to crank the engine manually.

Adventurous automobilists, meanwhile, were constantly blazing new trails and setting new records. These efforts further helped to popularize the new means of transportation. In the summer of 1903, for instance, the whole nation followed E. T. Fetch and M. C. Krarup as they successfully made the first coast-to-coast auto trip. The pair navigated a Packard Pacific from San Francisco to New York in fifty-two days, an awesomely fast trip for the era.

By 1910 the number of cars produced annually in America had grown to 187,000, and the number on the road was approaching half a million. Their popularity continued to explode in the next decade, and by 1917 five million cars were roaring down the nation's roads.

The Ford Era

At one time, hundreds of tiny companies turned out their own models of cars in factories that were often no bigger than a garage. Most of these independent companies have disappeared and been forgotten: the Apperson, the

Across America by Car

In the late summer of 1903, the whole nation followed the exploits of E. T. Fetch and M. C. Krarup, a pair of adventurers who succeeded in making the first coast-to-coast trip by automobile. They drove their Packard Pacific from San Francisco to New York in fifty-two days. The press repeatedly reassured the public that, despite this amazingly short time, the duo had many difficulties along the way. One stretch, according to a *Popular Mechanics* article reprinted in Walter Lord's *The Good Years*, "made the autoists think they had certainly strolled beyond the domains of human aggression. An indefatigable [unstoppable] perseverance and determination, however, successfully steered them out of this unearthly region." The bleak region in question, it turned out, was Utah.

Franklin, the Pierce Arrow, the Locomobile, the Stanley Steamer.

Others survived and prospered. Mack Truck, Chevrolet, and Oldsmobile are some of the names that have survived from the early days of motoring. In 1903, meanwhile, the most successful car manufacturer of all formed his own company.

Henry Ford was a Michigan farm boy who, like many young men, liked to tinker with machines. The Ford Motor Company was modestly successful in its first years, until Ford realized that the secret lay in creating a simple, reliable machine that anyone could afford.

In 1908 he introduced the Model T. The four-cylinder, ten-horsepower "tin lizzie" would eventually become the world's most famous car, but it did not catch on at first. Fewer than six thousand were sold the first year.

However, Ford was so convinced that he was on to something good that he announced the following year that his factory would manufacture only Model Ts, offering no other styles. His competitors thought the idea was crazy and predicted that Ford would go out of business within six months.

Instead, Model Ts began selling astronomically well, more than doubling every year. As production increased, Ford began cutting prices drastically. By 1916, more than half a million Model Ts had been sold and the price for a new touring car, the most popular version, had plummeted from its original price of $850 in 1908 to $360.

The Assembly Line

Ford's ability to increase production and decrease price was due, in part, to his experiments with assembly-line techniques for mass production. With the assembly line, Ford could cut the time needed for creating a car's chassis, for instance, from twelve and a half hours to one and a half hours.

The Model T, or "tin lizzie," would eventually become the most popular American car of the decade.

led to Ford's famous comment that Model T drivers could have any color car they wanted . . . as long as it was black.

Henry Ford did not invent the concept of the assembly line, but he did much to perfect it. He also helped popularize the technique's use among manufacturers of various other products, and the idea was adopted by a broad spectrum of industries. Ford's operating philosophy in time came to be a major influence on how American industry was run. Page Smith sums up Ford's contribution by remarking:

As a mechanic and inventor Henry Ford was hardly to be distinguished from other young men. Where he differed was in his vision of a nation of automobile owners driving a single standardized, inexpensive, and durable "universal car." . . . It was Ford's brilliant insight that cars might be produced not lovingly, one by one . . . but rather as one made galoshes or any other mass-produced item.[51]

Such techniques meant that Ford cars could be sold cheaply, but they also meant that all consumers got essentially the same machine. There was no such thing as custom-building. This situation

Rich and Poor on the Road

Cars had started out as the playthings of the rich. Spurred on by Ford's innovations in pricing, however, the automobile industry gradually began marketing to middle-class consumers as well as the wealthy.

Even though Henry Ford did much to make cars affordable to everyone, many still could not come up with the cash for one. Cars were still often coveted by the poor, for whom they were symbols of success and luxury.

On the other hand, to the working class, automobiles could also be sinister symbols of the idle rich. A future president, Woodrow Wilson, speaking in 1906 as the president of Princeton, remarked of automobiles, "To the countryman [farmer], they are the picture of the arrogance of wealth, with all its independence and carelessness." [52]

By the close of the Progressive era, automobiles were commonplace among middle-class families. Within a decade or so, the machines had made the transition from novelty to near necessity, just as telephones had already become almost essential in every middle-class home.

Increased mobility, whether in a car or through other forms of transportation, fit with America's view of itself as it strode into the twentieth century. The mood was one of expansion and movement. Frederick Lewis Allen comments, "Americans felt that a rolling stone gathers experience, adventure, sophistication, and—with luck—new and possibly fruitful opportunities." [53]

Some of those opportunities lay within America's borders. Others, however, existed in the outside world.

Chapter Six

Pictured is the Battle of Santiago, a naval battle that took place during the Spanish-American War. The war, which one writer deemed "splendid," helped the United States gain territory and become a global power.

America Abroad: Speaking Softly and Carrying a Big Stick

Compared to the great European powers, the United States was a relatively new and untested country late in the nineteeth century. America had not yet achieved full membership in the club of great world powers.

However, just before the turn of the century, the United States won a war and, for the first time, acquired land far outside its borders. This gave the country a new status among the world's dominant nations. During the 1900s, the country further tested and increased its role as a leader in global affairs.

Much of this new attitude was due to Theodore Roosevelt's aggressive leadership. Even before becoming president, Roosevelt had advocated a strong American presence on the world playing field. In a letter to a colleague dating from 1900, he had approvingly noted the country's robust aspects in foreign policy when he wrote that Americans "are becoming, owing to our strength and geographical situation, more and more the balance of power of the whole globe."[54]

Big Stick

One distinctive aspect of foreign affairs in previous centuries had been the phenomenon of widespread colonization. Large nations had controlled smaller, weaker foreign lands, creating trading arrangements that were favorable to themselves while excluding competitors. Primarily, this involved European countries controlling colonies in Asia, Africa, and South America.

The era of colonization was winding down, although several European powers, including Great Britain, Spain, France, and Germany, still maintained colonies. These powers were nearly always bickering with each other over various territorial disputes, and the threat of war was nearly always present.

Throughout the nineteenth century, America had maintained a strong isolationist policy in such disputes. That is,

it had chosen not to become involved in conflicts outside its boundaries. However, that policy changed as the new century began.

As with domestic policy, the tone of this newfound aggressive attitude was largely set by Theodore Roosevelt. During his administration he developed strong new policies of intervention in South America and the Pacific. He then backed up these policies with direct action, including establishing foreign territories, beginning construction on the Panama Canal, and sending a fleet of warships on a showy cruise around the world.

It was in foreign policy that Roosevelt best put to use his combination of soothing diplomatic language and the threat of military muscle. This attitude is famously expressed by his favorite declaration, borrowed from a West African proverb: "Speak softly and carry a big stick—you will go far."

War Brews

The single event that did the most to place America among the great world powers occurred late in the previous century: the Spanish-American War of 1898, the first conflict America fought on foreign soil.

Wars of independence had swept through Latin America during the nineteenth century, liberating many countries

Teddy Roosevelt carries his big stick across the Caribbean to help Cuba gain independence from Spain.

from the influence of Spain. By 1890, the islands of Cuba and Puerto Rico were all that remained of Spain's once extensive empire in the Americas.

The United States had always taken a strong interest in these two nearby islands. Their close proximity made them important from a military standpoint. They were also important economically, especially Cuba; American businessmen had invested heavily in the island's rich sugar and tobacco plantations, and American business presence there was strong.

For some time, tension had been mounting between the occupying Spaniards and Cuban revolutionaries battling for independence. By the mid-1890s, this became open conflict. Thousands of Cubans who had been branded as hostile were herded into "reconcentration" camps by Spanish troops. Hundreds of them died of exposure, hunger, and disease.

Popular sentiment in America ran high against these brutal conditions. The public's opinion was inflamed by sensational articles in newspapers owned by influential "yellow" publishers, especially Joseph Pulitzer and William Randolph Hearst.

Many members of the public as well as Congress called for American intervention in gaining Cuba's independence. They were also concerned about the welfare of Americans and American-owned property in the country. At first, President McKinley opposed the idea of sending American troops to Cuba. He hoped the conflict could be worked out without military force.

In December 1897, however, American citizens and property were threatened by riots in the capital city of Havana. McKinley reluctantly sent the battleship *Maine* there as a protective measure. Then tragedy struck: in February 1898, the *Maine* blew up while anchored in Havana Harbor and over 250 men died.

The Maine *enters Havana Harbor (above), only to be blown to pieces (right). Although history cannot identify what made the* Maine *explode, U.S. newspapers conveniently blamed Spain, helping to propel the Spanish-American War.*

"Remember the *Maine!*"

Responsibility for the explosion has never been fully determined. Some observers and historians have claimed it was the work of the Spanish; however, the Spanish government, which had a relatively weak military, was doing all it could to keep American intervention to a minimum. Others have blamed Cuban freedom fighters; the revolutionaries blew up the ship, according to this argument, to force America to enter the conflict. Another theory is that the explosion was simply a terrible accident stemming from an overheated boiler that ignited a store of ammunition.

In any event, the explosion triggered war. The Hearst and Pulitzer papers used the incident to inflame public opinion further, with lurid, illustrated articles detailing the tragedy. Congress was also outraged. "Remember the *Maine!* To hell with Spain!" became an often-heard catchphrase. Pressure to do something drastic mounted, and in April 1898, war was officially declared.

It was a dramatically one-sided war. Spain, already relatively weak and impoverished, had a woefully unprepared army and navy. The Spanish forces were no match for the Americans, especially the well-equipped U.S. Navy.

This was true not only in Cuba but in another Spanish territory, the Philippine Islands, on the other side of the world. In one of the first events of the war, Theodore Roosevelt, then undersecretary of the navy, sent a fleet under the command of Commodore George Dewey to Manila, the capital city of the Philippines.

Dewey's ships easily demolished the Spanish in Manila Bay. The Spanish lost their entire fleet and many men; American losses amounted to seven

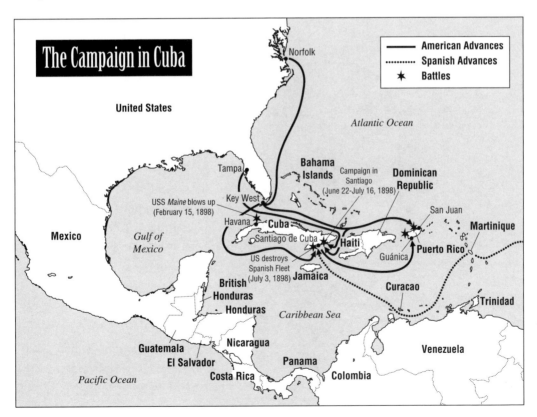

The Campaign in Cuba

— American Advances
········· Spanish Advances
★ Battles

Norfolk

United States

Atlantic Ocean

Tampa

Bahama Islands

Campaign in Santiago (June 22-July 16, 1898)

Dominican Republic

USS *Maine* blows up (February 15, 1898)

Key West

San Juan

Havana

Martinique

Mexico

Gulf of Mexico

Cuba

Santiago de Cuba

Haiti

Puerto Rico

US destroys Spanish Fleet (July 3, 1898)

Guánica

British Honduras

Jamaica

Curacao

Honduras

Caribbean Sea

Trinidad

Guatemala

Nicaragua

El Salvador

Panama

Venezuela

Pacific Ocean

Costa Rica

Colombia

slightly wounded sailors. An American military post was established in Manila, and by summer eleven thousand American troops were stationed throughout the Philippines.

Short War, New Land

Meanwhile, American warships were blockading Cuban waters and Ameri-

The Campaign in the Philippines

can infantry had landed ashore. These soldiers included a brigade of volunteers, the Rough Riders, enthusiastically led by Roosevelt himself.

American casualties were relatively few. American soldiers suffered more from tropical diseases, such as malaria, dysentery, and yellow fever, than they did from enemy bullets. All told, fewer than five hundred Americans died of wounds in the Philippines and Cuba, but over five thousand fell to fatal diseases.

Besides the victory in Manila Harbor, the war was highlighted by a rapid series of battles in Cuba, including Roosevelt's famous charge of San Juan Hill. Spanish forces greatly outnumbered those of America, but demoralized Spanish officers failed to press their advantage. In July, less than three months after the hostilities began, the Spanish government sued for peace and the war was over.

The problem then was what to do with what had once been Spanish lands. After extensive discussions, Spain agreed to grant Cuba independence. It also "sold" the entire Philippines to the United States for $20 million.

Roosevelt leads men up San Juan Hill in Cuba, in what would become one of the most famous battles of the Spanish-American War. Although greatly outnumbered by the Spanish, Roosevelt managed to intimidate them into surrendering for peace.

Furthermore, Spain gave the United States control over two of its other territories, Puerto Rico in the Caribbean and Guam in the South Pacific. These had been taken without a struggle; the Span-ish garrison in Guam had been so isolated that it had not even been aware that a war was on.

An American Empire?

The brief war both proved that the United States was a major military power and gave it an overseas empire. Americans, for the most part, rejoiced in the victory. The title of a popular book about the conflict, *A Splendid Little War*, summed up the general attitude.

The idea that America should have its own overseas empire had the approval of many citizens and politicians. The great European nations had colonies, these so-called expansionists argued; if the United States was to take its place among them, then it needed to match or surpass them.

In part, practical economics lent urgency to this new attitude. Newly settled land and improved farming methods were giving farmers the potential to produce food far beyond the needs of America's borders. America's manufacturing capacity was also exceeding domestic demand. The United States was competing as never before with other industrialized nations for shares in the world market and for raw materials.

The U.S. government was thus under pressure to find new avenues of trade. One solution was the possession of foreign land, or at least the possession of exclusive trading agreements with them. This would enlarge the supply of raw materials as well as markets for exports.

There was also an advantage, in terms of military strength, to having a presence in foreign lands. Overseas colonies could not only serve as ports for America's merchant fleet, but also for naval vessels that were needed to protect America's financial interests overseas.

Manifest Destiny

Another factor in the move for expansion was national pride. The term "manifest destiny" had been used since 1845 to signify the ideas that Americans were a special people, that their land was a special place, and that they had an almost religious mission to create a great country based on institutions such as republican government, individual liberty, and capitalism. After the continental United States had been more or less settled, many Americans began to extend this vision abroad.

If the United States was destined to be the greatest nation on earth, they reasoned, it was only natural for Americans to bring their government and way of life to others. This attitude was bolstered in part by the now discredited theory that people of northern European descent, especially those of English origin, were genetically superior to other races.

To expansionists, manifest destiny overseas was not a greedy campaign for power or an expression of ethnic superiority. It was a grandly moral crusade to remake the world for the better—a campaign waged by diplomats, merchants, industrialists, the military, and by religious and cultural missionaries.

This moral zeal was bolstered by Roosevelt's stern personal attitude. In his autobiography, written in 1913, he notes:

During the seven and a half years that I was President, this Nation behaved . . . toward all other nations precisely as an honorable man behaves to his fellow-men. We made no promise which we could not and did not keep. We made no threat which we did not carry out. We never failed to assert our rights in the face of the strong, and we never failed to treat both strong and weak with courtesy and justice; and against the weak when they misbehaved we were slower to assert our rights than we were against the strong.[55]

In Search of the Pole

In the 1900s, polar travel was as thrilling as space travel would become in later years. Exploration of the Poles, the only truly unexplored regions of the world, combined scientific and romantic fervor with the added spice of national rivalries. Commander Robert Peary's push to the North Pole symbolized America's bold, expansive territorial mood.

Peary had dreamed of being first to the Pole since first surveying Greenland as a naval officer. He was vain, uncompromising, and emotionally stiff, but he was also a brave and tireless explorer. Just as important, his enthusiasm for the Pole encouraged officials and backers to support his cause.

In July 1908, after several failed attempts, Peary and his team sailed from New York City on his ship *Roosevelt,* with crowds cheering and the presidential yacht booming a salute. The ship picked up a crew of Eskimos and dogs in Greenland, along with tons of whale meat for food.

After wintering in Cape Sheridan, Ellesmere Island, in February 1909, the polar party left: Peary, six assistants, and seventeen Eskimos, plus over a hundred dogs and nineteen sledges carrying 650 pounds of supplies apiece. This support team did much of the work along the way, allowing the pair who completed the journey, Peary and his longtime assistant Matthew Henson, to be well rested for the final push.

The journey was rough: even the brandy that Peary kept next to his chest remained frozen. However, by early April, with 133 miles to go, Peary and Henson left their colleagues behind. They reached the Pole on April 7, took celestial measurements to double-check their location, and raised several flags, including an American flag and a peace symbol.

Peary's return was both triumphant and a near-disaster. He received a hero's welcome, but a former colleague, Dr. Frederick Cook, soon returned from an expedition of his own, claiming that he had reached the Pole nearly a year before Peary.

Cook was a popular and likeable figure, unlike the aloof Peary, and many believed him. There was also ugly gossip about Henson, an African American. However, after lengthy debate, Cook's claim was disproved. Eskimos who had been with Cook refuted many details of his tale, and he lacked polar observations that would have proved his story. Furthermore, Cook's sled was barely scraped—not badly damaged as it would surely have been after such an arduous trip.

Peary was deeply hurt that he would be doubted, and remained bitter for the rest of his life. Nonetheless, he was made a rear admiral in 1911. In a comment reprinted in Walter Lord's *The Good Years,* Peary stated, "This work is the finish, the cap and the climax of nearly four hundred years of effort, loss of life, and expenditure of fortunes by the civilized nations of the world, and it has been accomplished in a way that is thoroughly American. I am content."

Isolationists

Not everyone was pleased, however. A small but vocal group of isolationists strongly opposed America's aggressive expansion.

Some of these isolationists felt that the war with Cuba, though cloaked in the guise of a morally justified crusade, had been unfairly fought to protect American business interests in Cuba. Some believed that holding power over noncitizens was cruel, unfair, and contrary to American principles. Still others feared that expansion could lead to "contamination" from supposedly inferior non-Caucasian races.

The isolationists also had a practical side to their argument. They pointed out that acquiring far-off territories would create enormous expenses, anger other countries, and inevitably lead to exhausting wars of independence. They noted that guerrillas in the Philippines were already waging war to keep American troops out of their land. This battle ended in 1902, but Americans remained in the islands and anti-American feelings continued to run high among the Filipinos.

No matter how isolationists and expansionists divided themselves, the Spanish-American War left a permanent mark on America. The experience changed forever how the United States regarded its place in the world. Its impact would be felt throughout the 1900s and far beyond. Fon Boardman Jr. writes, "No event of the last years of the old century did more to change the world for Americans than the Spanish-American War." [56]

China

One immediate outcome of America's presence in the Philippines was the stronger voice it gained in the political life of Asia, especially regarding the two major Asian countries, China and Japan. A forceful presence in the Pacific had been a priority for Roosevelt even before he became president. In a speech he made in 1900, he had remarked, "I wish to see the United States the dominant power on the shores of the Pacific Ocean." [57]

In China, the issue was mainly trade. China had long been an important center of Asian economics, and the United States was eager to gain access.

However, most of China's trade with the West had been with European firms that had taken advantage of its weak government to establish exclusive trading terms. In the 1890s, America had sought a so-called open-door policy. This was designed to guarantee access to Chinese ports and equal trading rights for all nations.

At the same time, antiforeign agitation within China was gaining strength.

The Fists of Righteous Harmony

One of the first tests of America's newfound international power, in the wake of the Spanish-American War, came in 1900. It was led by a Chinese secret society known as the Fists of Righteous Harmony, or the Boxers. This group sought to rid China of all foreign influence, under such mottoes as "Protect the country, destroy the foreigner."

The Boxers waged an increasingly bloody battle against foreigners and Chinese Christians, whom they considered "secondary" foreigners. In the summer of 1900, the Boxers forced the entire foreign diplomatic corps, representing such major trading partners as England, Russia, Germany, and France, to take refuge in the British embassy in Peking.

The Boxers then laid siege to the embassy. The nations whose diplomats were under siege quickly assembled a retaliatory force, to which the United States contributed twenty-five hundred men. This group was successful in dispersing the Boxers and lifting the siege.

U.S. secretary of state John Hay used the victory to urge China and its trading partners to extend the open-door policy. This was Hay's plan to open China to free trade, including trade with the United States, while preserving China's territorial and administrative integrity and independence—that is, without carving up the giant country. Hay's plan proved effective

U.S. infantry line up before the Sacred Gate in Peking, China, to help quell the Boxer Rebellion. The United States used the victory over the Boxers to help usher in a more open trade policy with China.

to a degree, although America's ability to trade freely with China was never fully exploited. The advent of World War I put Hay's ambitious open-door policy on hold indefinitely.

They resented the longtime presence of Western traders, particularly the British. The most powerful of the anti-foreign groups was the secret Society of Righteous Fists, or "Boxers," as they were commonly called in the West. This agitation eventually took the form of open conflict.

In 1900 the Boxers gained control of Peking and besieged its foreign population, which took refuge in the British embassy. A multinational military force, including twenty-five hundred American soldiers, freed the foreigners and drove the Boxers out of Peking. It was a convincing display of American military force.

Japan

Concerning Japan, the question was not so much a trade issue as a complex game of balancing power among countries.

Japan and another country, Russia, had clear ambitions to expand their holdings in Asia. When war broke out between Japan and Russia in 1904 over a disputed group of islands between the two nations, the United States took the opportunity to have a hand in the politics of Asia. This was especially true when the Japanese won a spectacular victory and Roosevelt was asked to mediate a settlement. Roosevelt's success at this task earned him the Nobel Peace Prize in 1906.

Despite this collaborative success, relations between Japan and the United States were strained. In 1907, as anti-Japanese immigrant feeling rose in America, the situation became especially tense.

Roosevelt was able to defuse the situation somewhat with his "gentlemen's agreement" limiting Japanese immigration. However, he did not want this agreement to appear to be a sign of American weakness, because he worried about the threat of the growing Japanese military. He wrote in a letter to a colleague, "I am . . . anxious that they [the Japanese government] would realize that I am not afraid of them and that the United States will no more submit to bullying than it will to bully."[58]

Late in 1907 Roosevelt launched a spectacular display of his "big stick" policy. He sent sixteen powerful new battleships, called the Great White Fleet because of the color they were painted, on an unprecedented forty-five-thousand-mile voyage around the world. Many saw this move as a deliberate show of strength, a "big stick" warning, toward Japan.

The Great White Fleet

Officially the voyage was a goodwill mission that would also serve to give the navy experience in sailing its new ships in close formation. Unofficially, it was a show of American naval strength. The ships were a visible symbol, to the nation and the world, of Roosevelt's belief that America needed to maintain a navy as powerful as those of any other country.

The fleet was well received everywhere, with thousands crowding the waterfront to cheer its arrival in every city. After leaving the East Coast, the fleet first visited South America. On the West Coast of America and in Hawaii, cities lobbied fiercely for the honor of having the fleet sail into their ports. Lavish balls, dinners, and receptions were held in the lucky cities.

Around the World

The fleet continued its journey to the Philippines and Japan. Despite some uncertainty beforehand, the Americans were warmly greeted in both places. At Tokyo's waterfront, ten thousand schoolchildren sang "Hail Columbia" and fifty thousand Tokyoites took part in a celebratory torchlight parade.

One evening, the American sailors endeared themselves to the Japanese through an act of personal bravery. During a nighttime ceremony, a flimsy wooden archway caught fire and the Japanese flag at the top was in danger of burning. A group of American sailors and marines climbed to the top

of the burning structure and saved the Japanese flag. The crowd cheered wildly, a welcome finish to what could have been a touchy occasion.

After continuing through the Suez Canal and the Mediterranean, the ships arrived back in America by the end of February, some fourteen months after leaving.

The voyage served its purpose; the combination of expressed goodwill and implied threat helped forge an understanding, at least temporarily, between Japan and America. By the time the ships returned home, Japan had agreed to support America's open-door policy in China and to support America's overall role in the Pacific. The United States, meanwhile, quietly agreed to give Japan a free hand in the Chinese province of Manchuria, where its rivalry with Russia continued.

Roosevelt felt the mutual understanding achieved by the Great White Fleet was one of his most significant achievements in world politics. He later remarked, "In my own judgment the most important service that I rendered to peace was the voyage of the battle fleet round the world."[59]

A Man, a Plan, a Canal: Panama

Engineers, politicians, and businessmen had long dreamed of a Central

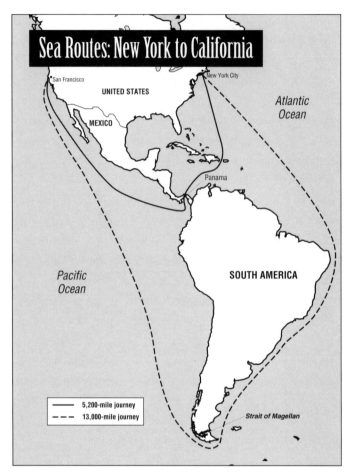

Sea Routes: New York to California

San Francisco
New York City
UNITED STATES
Atlantic Ocean
MEXICO
Panama
Pacific Ocean
SOUTH AMERICA

— 5,200-mile journey
- - - 13,000-mile journey

Strait of Magellan

foreign policy toward the nations of the Western Hemisphere in the 1900s.

In the previous century, a French company had tried to dig a canal across the narrow isthmus of Panama, which was then a province of Colombia. However, the firm had gone bankrupt. A commission appointed by Roosevelt to explore the question recommended that a new canal be built at the same location as this abandoned French project.

The United States first tried to negotiate a treaty with Colombia that would give America the right to build and operate a canal in Panama. However, the Colombian government rejected the proposal, which they felt would give them too little money and power over the affair. Roosevelt, furious, complained in a letter to a colleague, "You could no more make an agreement with the Colombian rulers than you could nail currant jelly to a wall."[60]

American canal connecting the Atlantic and the Pacific Oceans. Without a connecting canal, ships traveling from one American coast to the other had to make a long and arduous trip around the tip of South America.

As America's military and trade interests in the Pacific expanded, creating such a canal became an even higher priority. The effort it took to get the Panama Canal under way was the most dramatic aspect of America's assertive

Panama Revolts

Roosevelt considered seizing Panama by force, but this proved unnecessary.

Late in 1903, Panamanians launched a successful revolt against Colombia. The uprising had the backing of the American government, which provided troops to keep the Colombians from quashing it. The revolt was short and definitive; the only casualties were one dog and one man.

Within weeks the United States, recognizing Panama as an independent country, was granted the right to build and operate a canal and to control a strip of land called the Canal Zone. Work began almost immediately and continued until 1914.

The canal was an enormously complex project, but for the most part it proceeded smoothly. The engineering aspects were enough of a challenge, but the American team also had to combat the threat of such deadly tropical diseases as malaria and yellow fever.

Fortunately, thanks to new discoveries in preventing the spread of tropical disease, there were virtually no deadly outbreaks during construction. Furthermore, the causes of these diseases, including swamplands that fostered the breeding of mosquitoes, were almost completely eliminated in the region.

The engineering and medical successes associated with the canal were extensively reported, and they filled most Americans with pride. The project even gave rise to a famous palindrome, a phrase that reads the same backward and forward: A man, a plan, a canal: Panama.

However, some Americans were ashamed of the ruthless actions taken to gain Panama. They condemned what they saw as America's high-handed role in taking what it wanted.

Roosevelt repeatedly asserted that his actions were justified in the interests of Latin American peace and stability. America's actions were, he declared, "in accordance with the highest, finest, and nicest standards of public and governmental ethics." He also maintained that the United States had not actively

The Panama Canal, viewed during the construction phase.

supported the revolt in Panama. However, in 1911 he could not resist boasting, "I took the Canal Zone and let Congress debate; and while the debate goes on the Canal does also."[61]

The Roosevelt Corollary

Roosevelt's policy toward European countries generally maintained America's traditional neutrality. However, his main concern was with the defense of the United States. On occasion, he vigorously challenged European nations if their actions seemed to threaten America.

In time, this policy soon expanded to include aggression toward America's neighbors in the Caribbean and Central and South America. If a European country acted in the Western Hemisphere in a way that seemed to threaten America or its neighbors, Roosevelt did not hesitate to respond.

One such incident was Germany's naval blockade of Venezuela in 1902–1903, an effort to force that country to pay some long-delinquent debts. Roosevelt ordered an American fleet to go on protective maneuvers in the Caribbean and warned the German authorities that he would use force if Germany used the opportunity to acquire territory.

Wanting to avoid a violent incident, the Germans agreed to hold talks that would resolve the situation. Roosevelt's threat did the trick of turning the Germans back. Page Smith comments wryly, "The only gobbling up in the Western Hemisphere would be done by the United States."[62]

As a result of this incident, in 1904 Roosevelt formulated a plan explicitly expanding the U.S. role as "policeman." The Roosevelt Corollary to the Monroe Doctrine, as it came to be called, stated

MORE TROUBLE FOR THE INTERNATIONAL POLICEMAN

Theodore Roosevelt exercises his right to become involved in Central American affairs. Roosevelt was one of the first to articulate that Central American nations were in the U.S. sphere of influence.

outright that America reserved the right to intervene in the internal affairs of Latin American and Caribbean nations to insure the region's peace and stability.

No nation, the policy asserted, should be allowed to interfere in the affairs of these countries as long as they behaved decently and remained stable. However, Roosevelt added, "brutal wrongdoing, or an impotence which results in a general loosening of the ties of civilized society, may finally require intervention by some civilized nation, and . . . the United States cannot ignore this duty."[63]

In this and other vigorous foreign policies, Roosevelt proved that he was, in some ways, even stronger and less willing to compromise than he was on the domestic front. His aggressive pursuit of American ideals and policies helped move the nation forward onto the world stage, into the hands of a new president and a new decade.

Chapter Seven

Madison Square Garden is dramatically lit in this period etching. The electrification of street lighting helped spur an increase in nighttime activities.

Summary: The Decade Ends

Both at home and abroad, America saw enormous changes, as well as the promise of more to come, during the first decade of the twentieth century. In many ways, these changes were caused by the country's significant problems. At the same time, America showed great optimism that these problems could be solved.

The End Draws Near

As the end of the decade drew near, difficulties still plagued many aspects of life. The gap between the rich and the poor was still great. Proper education for all was still only a dream. Corruption in government, in cities and states as well as on the federal level, was still widespread.

Working conditions were terrible for many, including the large numbers of children in factories and on farms. Crippling strikes, some of them violent, underscored the problems between organized labor and business. Diseases such as influenza and cholera were still common, due in part to such factors as inadequate diet, poor medical training, and unregulated medications. And many people, especially recent immigrants in tenement buildings, still lived in appalling and dangerous conditions.

At the same time, there was hope that many of the nation's most pressing issues could be solved. To a large degree, this optimism proved warranted as the decade drew to a close. The reform movements that swept the nation, for instance, did much to alleviate the problems of the poor and disadvantaged. Reformers also worked hard to clean up corrupt government bureaucracies.

The technological changes that took place during the decade also created dramatic changes. Some of these new inventions had been created earlier, but their widespread acceptance occurred during the 1900s. The automobile, the telephone, electric lights,

The Quake

Several disasters struck America during the 1900s, including a hurricane and tidal wave along the Texas coast in 1900 that killed 6,000 and a fire at Chicago's Iroquois Theater that killed 602 in 1903. None, however, compared in long-lasting impact with the earthquake that devastated San Francisco, then the foremost city on America's West Coast.

It struck on the morning of April 18, 1906, and lasted less than a minute. Many large buildings, including City Hall and the lavish opera house, collapsed immediately. More damaging than the quake itself, however, was the fire that followed.

In the end, nearly five hundred square blocks were destroyed. Twenty-five thousand buildings had collapsed or lay in ashes. Four hundred and fifty people were dead, thousands were injured, and nearly a quarter of a million were homeless.

Rebuilding began immediately. The federal government provided millions in relief funds, bakers in Los Angeles sent twenty-five thousand loaves of bread a day, and entertainers like the famous actress Sarah Bernhardt helped raise money for the stricken city.

Authorities respectfully declined offers of help from other countries. They were eager to show that Americans could care for their own. About this confident determination, which could be said to characterize the decade as a whole, historian Walter Lord writes in his book *The Good Years*, "It was not the decision of a country with an inferiority complex."

and appliances such as vacuum cleaners that made daily life easier, would dramatically affect American life well into the future.

"A Little Bit Taller"

To many people at the time, and to many historians today, the decade of the 1900s was symbolized by one man. Teddy Roosevelt was, far and away, the dominant figure in the life of the United States during the 1900s. He was also the first really strong president of modern America.

The reforms of the Progressive movement were immensely helped by Roosevelt's robust support. His trust-busting activities broke the backs of many unethical business practices. His active role in mediating between labor unions and business leaders helped the two groups solve their differences. His support of regulatory laws like the Pure Food and Drug Act aided in establishing new standards for consumer goods.

Roosevelt's aggressive foreign policy also did much to place America among the ranks of world powers, acquire overseas land, and launch the building of the Panama Canal. Furthermore, his concern for conservation of natural re-

Theodore Roosevelt tries his hand at a steam shovel during the building of the Panama Canal in 1906. The completion of the canal was a triumph for Roosevelt and the United States.

sources and the preservation of wilderness led to the protection of vast tracts of land for future generations.

All this made Roosevelt one of the best known and most admired individuals of his day. Not since Lincoln had a public figure been praised by so many. Typical was the praise of journalist Cecil Spring Rice when Roosevelt visited England: "Roosevelt has turned us all upside down. He has enjoyed himself hugely, and I must say [that] by the side of our statesmen, he looks a little bit taller, bigger, and stronger."[64]

Roosevelt's Departure from Office

However, the era during which Roosevelt dominated American life was drawing to a close. By late 1907, he had decided not to run for another term in the 1908 election.

The constitutional amendment limiting presidents to two terms had not yet been passed. Nonetheless, it had always been the custom for presidents to step down after two terms, and Roosevelt publicly announced that he would honor the custom.

In many ways, he said, he felt that his work was done. He told a newspaper editor:

> There was crusading to do when I took hold. There was something that had to be uprooted. . . . The conscience of business had to be aroused, the authority of the government over big as well as small had to be asserted. You can't half do that kind of job; it must be done thoroughly. I think I've done it. I didn't use a feather duster. I knew I had to hit hard—and be hit hard in return. We have had four years of uprooting and four years of crusading. The country has had enough of it and of me.[65]

A New President Is Chosen

Roosevelt would surely have been elected again if he so chose. Instead, he carefully examined the men he considered worthy successors, looking for someone who would continue the policies he had begun.

Roosevelt's longtime colleague Elihu Root, most recently his secretary of state, was a strong contender.

Joy in Office

Theodore Roosevelt infuriated many politicians and voters. But for the most part Roosevelt's personal energy and sense of fun delighted the nation. An adviser recalls a meeting that was delayed because Roosevelt's six children were fending off an imaginary attack by Indians, and the nation's leader was lowering them by rope from a second story window. Toward the end of his term of office, in a comment reprinted in Time-Life's *1900–1910*, Roosevelt remarked, "I don't think that any family has ever enjoyed the White House more than we have."

Roosevelt's good-humored vitality set the mood of the country in the 1900s. Not until another Roosevelt became president, his distant relative Franklin, would the country have such a dynamic and popular leader. Page Smith's *America Enters the World* reprints a comment from William Allen White, a prominent newspaper editor of the time: "The gift of the gods to TR was joy, joy in life."

However, Root's health was uncertain, and his close ties to the Wall Street banking establishment made him a dubious choice.

Roosevelt instead picked his secretary of war, William Howard Taft. Taft was an able administrator who had served the country well in a variety of posts. He was also an amiable man who got along well with nearly everyone. However, he was in many ways an odd choice. For one thing, he was in some ways the opposite of Roosevelt. He was not an intellectual, and did not care for the relentless and varied learning that characterized Roosevelt's style.

Also, unlike the compulsively energetic Roosevelt, Taft disliked physical exercise. He was so overweight that he once got stuck in a White House bathtub and had to be extricated by members of his Secret Service staff. Furthermore, he disliked the intensely public world of politics. "I don't like politics," he wrote to a friend. "I don't like the limelight."[66]

Taft Takes Over

Taft really desired to be a Supreme Court justice. However, his ambitious wife urged him to accept Roosevelt's suggestion that he run for the presidency. Historians Oscar Theodore Barck Jr. and Nelson Manfred Blake write, "Yielding to both presidential and family pressure, Taft agreed to seek the White House instead of the Supreme Court post that would have been his own preference."[67]

In the 1908 election, Taft easily defeated the Democratic nominee, William Jennings Bryan. As his successor took over the reins of office early in 1909, Roosevelt prepared to leave on an extended African safari. He had led the country for nearly the entire decade, and he was ready for a

TR's Advice

Roosevelt offered considerable advice to William Howard Taft, his chosen successor as president, as Taft prepared to campaign for the office.

"Let the audience see you smile always," Roosevelt wrote, as quoted in Walter Lord's *The Good Years*. He further advised special care when photographers were present while one was relaxing with sports:

"The folly of mankind is difficult to fathom; it would seem incredible that anyone would care one way or the other about your playing golf, but I have received literally hundreds of letters from the west protesting about it. . . .

"I myself play tennis, but that game is a little more familiar; besides, you never saw a photograph of me playing tennis. I'm careful about that; photographs on horseback, yes; tennis, no. And golf is fatal."

change. In a whimsical mood, the departing chief wrote to his successor, "Ha! Ha! *You* are making up your Cabinet. *I* in a light-hearted way have spent the morning testing the rifles for my African trip."[68]

Many politicians and members of the public were sorry to see the charismatic and effective Roosevelt leave office. Not everyone was regretful, however. When informed of Roosevelt's impending African trip, his old enemy J. P. Morgan allegedly proclaimed, "Health to the lions."

In some areas, Taft ably continued and expanded Roosevelt's policies. He expanded America's land to include new states, including New Mexico and Arizona. He also created two important government agencies that helped "ordinary" people, the parcel post system and the postal savings bank, which provided a convenient and safe way for poorer people to deposit their money in a bank operated by the post office.

Furthermore, he laid important groundwork for innovations such as copyright law, the first income tax, and direct voting for Senate seats. He instituted several important antitrust suits, continued to support large-scale irrigation projects, and tightened regulations of big businesses such as railroads.

Roosevelt handpicked his secretary of war, William Howard Taft, to run for president as his successor. Roosevelt later became disenchanted with Taft.

A Flap over Conservation

In other ways, however, Taft drifted away from Roosevelt's policies. The issue that aroused the greatest outcry from Progressivists involved conservation and natural resources. Although the U.S. Agriculture Department continued to be the world's leading research establishment in its field, it became involved in a bitter and scandalous political struggle.

Roosevelt's longtime ally, forestry director Gifford Pinchot, was dissatisfied with the Taft administration. Taft favored a more traditional approach to government bureaucracy than had Roosevelt. As a result, Pinchot did not have as free a hand as before in regulating natural resources.

A crisis occurred when Pinchot accused Taft's secretary of the interior, Richard A. Ballinger, of unethical dealings. Ballinger had close ties to lumber and mining interests in the Pacific Northwest, and Pinchot publicly accused him of favoring those interests.

A dramatic view of the Grand Canyon. Taft's administration was dogged by a controversy over government contracts to use natural resources.

Taft was outraged at Pinchot and summarily fired him.

The congressional investigation into the matter captured headlines for several months. In the end it created significant political damage on both sides. The conservation movement lost some of the power it had enjoyed under Roosevelt, and Pinchot lost much of his influence. Forestry historian Harold K. Steen writes, "Much more would be accomplished subsequently, of course, but never again would a single figure be so dominant."[69]

Other Reforms Move Ahead

Elsewhere, reform efforts moved ahead as the decade drew to a close.

More and more states went "dry" as the temperance movement achieved more influence. Eventually, the movement succeeded in establishing a nationwide prohibition of alcohol that lasted from 1920 to 1933.

Child labor activists who had done so much during the 1900s also scored successes in future decades. By 1914, most states had passed minimum-age laws, usually fourteen. In 1916 a national law to regulate child labor was passed, but this law was declared unconstitutional two years later. It would be many years before comprehensive and lasting legislation would be passed.

An early temperance poster touts the advantages to remaining sober. The temperance movement gained momentum during the 1900s.

In foreign policy, America's strong hand continued, even as tensions in Europe mounted toward the beginning of World War I in 1914. It was up to Taft's successor, Woodrow Wilson, to lead the United States into that battle. Work on the Panama Canal progressed, meanwhile, until its completion in 1914.

Altogether, as the first decade of the century ended, despite some disappointments, the spirit of reform was still in the air. The reforms carried out during that first decade had an impact that is still felt; Roosevelt's insistence on a strong and active government dedicated to creating a Square Deal for everyone set the tone for many future administrations.

Indeed, it is difficult to imagine modern America without the reforms, or the governmental policies, that were set during the 1900s. Frederick Lewis Allen comments, "It is hard for us, today, to realize how small the government was in 1900, and how limited its functions and powers."[70]

The Decade Ends

And so the decade ended. In the summer of 1910 Roosevelt returned from his lengthy African safari, convinced that his policies had been twisted by a hand-picked successor he had thought he could trust. Unable to resist jumping back into politics, Roosevelt would run again for president, unsuccessfully, in 1912.

Also in 1910, Halley's Comet appeared in the sky and dazzled millions of observers. The same year witnessed the death of the writer many consider the quintessential American author, Mark Twain.

Furthermore, the year 1910 was marked by the election of a future

As the decade ended, the year 1910 heralded both the appearance of Halley's Comet and the death of American writer Mark Twain.

One of America's most popular presidents, Franklin D. Roosevelt, would be elected to his first office in the New York State Senate in 1910.

president to his first office: Teddy Roosevelt's distant relative, young Franklin Delano Roosevelt, won a seat in the New York state senate. He was, significantly, the first politician ever to campaign by automobile. Teddy Roosevelt's ideals of Progressivism and the Square Deal would be echoed in the 1930s, when the second President Roosevelt used a massive government reform effort, the New Deal, to bring America out of a devastating depression.

Notes

Introduction:
A Century Begins

1. Quoted in Frederick Lewis Allen, *The Big Change*. New York: Harper, 1952, p.3.
2. Oscar Theodore Barck Jr. and Nelson Manfred Blake. *Since 1900*, New York: Macmillan, 1965, p. 126.
3. Quoted in Page Smith, *America Enters the World*. New York: Mc-Graw-Hill, 1985, p. 840.
4. Quoted in Frank Freidel, *America in the Twentieth Century*. New York: Knopf, 1960, p. 59.

Chapter One
Daily Life: In the Good
Old Summertime

5. Dorothy Schneider and Carl J. Schneider, *American Women in the Progressive Era, 1900–1920*. New York: Anchor/Doubleday, 1994, p. 7.
6. Walter Lord, *The Good Years*. New York: Harper, 1960, p. 107.
7. Freidel, *America in the Twentieth Century*, p. 42.
8. Allen, *The Big Change*, p. 10.
9. Fon W. Boardman Jr., *America and the Progressive Era, 1900–1917*. New York: Henry Z. Walck, 1970, p. 49.

10. Quoted in Smith, *America Enters the World*, pp. 1015–16.
11. Freidel, *America in the Twentieth Century*, p. 164.
12. Quoted in George E. Mowry, *The Era of Theodore Roosevelt*. New York: Harper & Row, 1958, pp. 1–2.

Chapter Two:
Social Problems, Social Cures:
The Birth of the Square Deal

13. Richard Hofstadter, *The Age of Reform*. New York: Knopf, 1961, p. 212.
14. Quoted in Iwan W. Morgan and Neil A. Wynn, eds., *America's Century*. New York: Holmes & Meier, 1993, p. 4.
15. Quoted in Hofstadter, *The Age of Reform*, p. 205.
16. Quoted in Michael Lesy, *Dreamland*. New York: The New Press, 1997, p. 108.
17. Quoted in Freidel, *America in the Twentieth Century*, p. 56.
18. Quoted in Allen, *The Big Change*, p. 57.
19. Quoted in Ezra Bowen and the Editors of Time-Life Books, *1900–1910*. New York: Time-Life Books, 1969, p. 84.

20. Freidel, *America in the Twentieth Century*, p. 47.

21. Barck and Blake, *Since 1900*, p. 129.

22. Frederick C. Howe, "The City," in Otis Pease, ed., *The Progressive Years*. New York: George Braziller, 1962, p. 51.

23. Mowry, *The Era of Theodore Roosevelt*, p. 59.

24. Quoted in Bowen and the Editors of Time-Life Books, *1900–1910*, p. 82.

25. Pease, ed., *The Progressive Years*, p. 14

26. William A. Link and Arthur S. Link, *American Epoch: A History of the United States Since 1900: Volume 1: War, Reform and Society 1900–45*. New York: McGraw-Hill, 1993, p. 54.

27. Quoted in Schneider, *American Women in the Progressive Era, 1900–1920*, p. 94.

Chapter Three:
Big Business, Labor, and
Trust Busting: An Era of Reform

28. Quoted in Freidel, *America in the Twentieth Century*, p. 4.

29. Barck and Blake, *Since 1900*, p. 12.

30. Quoted in Smith, *America Enters the World*, p. 151.

31. Quoted in Boardman, *America and the Progressive Era, 1900–1917*, p. 17.

32. Mowry, *The Era of Theodore Roosevelt*, p. 140.

33. Quoted in Freidel, *America in the Twentieth Century*, pp. 62–63.

34. Quoted in Lord, *The Good Years*, p. 82.

35. Quoted in Hofstadter, *The Age of Reform*, p. 233.

36. Quoted in Mowry, *The Era of Theodore Roosevelt*, p. 131.

Chapter Four:
Saving the Wilderness and
Settling the Land

37. Quoted in Edward B. Weinstock, *The Wilderness War*. New York: Julian Messner, 1982, p. 71.

38. Weinstock, *The Wilderness War*, p. 61.

39. Mowry, *The Era of Theodore Roosevelt*, p. 214.

40. Quoted in Donald J. Pisani, *Water, Land, and Law in the West*. Lawrence: University Press of Kansas, 1996, pp. 186–87.

41. Jonathan Raban, *Bad Land*. New York: Vintage/Random House, 1997, p. 180.

42. Charles F. Wilkinson, *The Eagle Bird: Mapping a New West*. New York: Vintage Books, 1993, p. 49.

43. Allen, *The Big Change*, p. 117.

44. Quoted in Pease, ed., *The Progressive Years*, p. 258.

Chapter Five:
Transportation Transformed:
The Automobile Age Begins

45. Schneider, *American Women in the Progressive Era, 1900–1920*, p. 241.

46. Link, *American Epoch*, p. 5.

47. Quoted in Lord, *The Good Years*, p. 88.

48. Allen, *The Big Change*, p. 119.

49. Smith, *America Enters the World*, p. 873.

50. Quoted in Lord, *The Good Years*, p. 116.

51. Smith, *America Enters the World*, p. 867.

52. Quoted in Bowen and the Editors of Time-Life Books, *1900–1910*, p. 236.

53. Allen, *The Big Change*, p. 129.

Chapter Six
America Abroad: Speaking Softly and Carrying a Big Stick

54. Quoted in Mowry, *The Era of Theodore Roosevelt*, p. 148.

55. Quoted in Pease, ed., *The Progressive Years*, p. 388.

56. Boardman, *America and the Progressive Era, 1900–1917*, p. 5.

57. Quoted in Mowry, *The Era of Theodore Roosevelt*, p. 146.

58. Quoted in Barck and Blake, *Since 1900*, p. 104.

59. Quoted in Pease, ed., *The Progressive Years*, p. 413.

60. Quoted in Smith, *America Enters the World*, p. 53.

61. Quoted in Freidel, *America in the Twentieth Century*, p. 127.

62. Smith, *America Enters the World*, p. 41.

63. Quoted in Boardman, *America and the Progressive Era, 1900–1917*, p. 70.

Chapter Seven
Summary: The Decade Ends

64. Quoted in Lord, *The Good Years*, p. 263.

65. Quoted in Smith, *America Enters the World*, p. 184.

66. Quoted in Mowry, *The Era of Theodore Roosevelt*, p. 233.

67. Barck and Blake, *Since 1900*, p. 61.

68. Quoted in Lord, *The Good Years*, p. 225.

69. Harold K. Steen in William Whyte, ed., *Our American Land*. Washington, DC: U.S. Government Printing Office, 1987, p. 174.

70. Allen, *The Big Change*, p. 81.

Chronology

1900

Boxer Rebellion in China begins, America sends troops to help restore order.

First system of running a city by commission established in Galveston, Texas.

1901

William McKinley assassinated, Theodore Roosevelt becomes president.

U.S. Steel, largest trust of era, organized.

First oil wells in Texas drilled.

Cuba becomes a protectorate of the United States.

Booker T. Washington's invitation to the White House creates an uproar.

1902

Coal strike in Pennsylvania threatens nation, becomes first incidence of federal intervention in labor dispute.

First muckraking articles investigating social ills appear.

Newlands Reclamation Act passed to aid settlement of arid western lands.

1903

Department of Commerce and Labor established.

Elkins Act regarding railroads in interstate commerce is passed.

Ford Motor Company organized.

First World Series played.

Wright brothers make first successful heavier-than-air flight.

Call of the Wild published.

First narrative film, *The Great Train Robbery,* released.

Panama revolts against Colombia with backing of United States, Canal Zone is placed under U.S. jurisdiction.

Pelican Island in Florida named first national wildlife refuge.

1904

Northern Securities Company v. United States: "trust-busting" prosecution of railroad holding company is successful.

Russo-Japanese War breaks out.

Roosevelt wins full second term as president.

Roosevelt Corollary announced.

Louisiana Purchase Exposition held in St. Louis.

1905

Swift and Company v. United States: successful prosecution of the beef trust.

Russo-Japanese War ends, Roosevelt mediates peace.

Industrial Workers of the World (IWW) organized.

Roosevelt begins second term.

Major construction work begins on Panama Canal.

1906

Passage of Hepburn Act strengthening the Interstate Commerce Commission.

Passage of Pure Food and Drug Act and Meat Inspection Act.

U.S. troops occupy Cuba to quell revolt.

Philippine revolution suppressed.

Devil's Tower in Wyoming named first national monument.

Lacey Antiquities Act, protecting ancient lands, passed.

Earthquake strikes San Francisco.

Roosevelt awarded Nobel Peace Prize for his role in mediating Russo-Japanese War.

1907

Roosevelt bars Japanese immigration.

Great White Fleet begins tour.

1908

Aldrich-Vreeland Act passes, regulating banking industry.

White House Conservation Conference held; National Commission for the Conservation of Natural Resources appointed by President Roosevelt.

William Howard Taft elected President.

Model T Ford introduced to public.

1909

NAACP is founded.

Taft takes office.

Expanded Homestead Act passed, aiding in settlement of the West.

1910

Passage of Mann-Elkins Act placing interstate communications system under the jurisdiction of the Interstate Commerce Commission.

For Further Reading

Janice Greene, *Our Century 1900–1910*. Belmont, CA: Fearon Education, 1989. Written in magazine style, this publication gives a brief and simple overview of some of the main events and people important in world history during the decade.

William Loren Katz, *From the Progressive Era to the Great Depression 1900–29*. New York: Franklin Watts, 1974. Focuses on the role of minorities in America during the first part of the century.

Zachary Kent, *Theodore Roosevelt: Twenty-Sixth President of the United States*. Chicago: Childrens Press, 1988. A well-illustrated biography of the man who helped shape the decade.

Hal Morgan and Andreas Brown, *Prairie Fires and Paper Moons: The American Photographic Postcard 1900–1920*. Boston: David R. Godine, 1981. A fascinating book with almost no text that reproduces picture postcards, often made for individuals, from the early part of the century.

Gail B. Stewart, *1900s*. New York: Crestwood House, 1989. Part of the Timelines series, this is a handy year-by-year accounting of the decade's major events.

Nancy Whitelaw, *Theodore Roosevelt Takes Charge*. Morton Grove, IL: Albert Whitman, 1992. A very thorough biography.

Works Consulted

Frederick Lewis Allen, *The Big Change*. New York: Harper, 1952. This excellent anecdotal history by a well-known popular historian looks at how changes in American culture during the first half of this century affected individuals.

Oscar Theodore Barck Jr. and Nelson Manfred Blake, *Since 1900*. New York: Macmillan, 1965. A densely written and scholarly look at the twentieth century by two professors of history.

Fon W. Boardman Jr., *America and the Progressive Era, 1900–1917*. New York: Henry Z. Walck, 1970. This history, which concentrates on the twentieth century up to the end of World War I, is concise and simply written.

Ezra Bowen and the Editors of Time-Life Books, *1900–1910*. New York: Time-Life Books, 1969. A well-illustrated and well-written overview, part of the series entitled *This Fabulous Decade*. Its focus is on social life, not economics or politics.

Frank Freidel, *America in the Twentieth Century*. New York: Knopf, 1960. A detailed but extremely readable one-volume history by a distinguished scholar of modern America.

Richard Hofstadter, *The Age of Reform*. New York: Knopf, 1961. This book by a well-regarded historian focuses on the Progressive movement.

Michael Lesy, *Dreamland*. New York: The New Press, 1997. A fascinating collection of photographs from the first decade of the century, with a brief accompanying timeline, that provides an excellent sense of the decade's mood.

William A. Link and Arthur S. Link, *American Epoch: A History of the United States Since 1900: Volume 1: War, Reform and Society 1900–45*. New York: McGraw-Hill, 1993. This revised edition is one volume of a classic college text on American history; extremely dry but densely packed with information.

Walter Lord, *The Good Years*. New York: Harper, 1960. An anecdotal and entertaining history of the twentieth century until World War I. Each chapter is devoted to a particular incident, such as the San Francisco earthquake and Peary's trek to the North Pole.

Iwan W. Morgan and Neil A. Wynn, eds., *America's Century*. New York: Holmes & Meier, 1993. A scholarly series of articles on twentieth-century American history. The editors and contributors are British professors of American history.

George E. Mowry, *The Era of Theodore Roosevelt*. New York: Harper & Row, 1958. This informative and lively book by a professor of American history focuses on Roosevelt's politics and policies.

Otis Pease, ed., *The Progressive Years*. New York: George Braziller, 1962. An excellent collection of writings by eminent men and women who helped shape the era, including Teddy Roosevelt, Jane Addams, and Lincoln Steffens, edited by a well-respected expert on American history.

Donald J. Pisani, *Water, Land, and Law in the West*. Lawrence: University Press of Kansas, 1996. This is a scholarly look at the history of water rights and public irrigation projects from the mid-1800s to the 1920s.

Jonathan Raban, *Bad Land*. New York: Vintage/Random House, 1997. A paperback edition of a 1996 book by a well-known British-born writer, this is a beautifully written and insightful exploration of the homesteading of the Plains in the early part of the century.

Dorothy Schneider and Carl J. Schneider, *American Women in the Progressive Era, 1900–1920*. New York: Anchor/Doubleday, 1994. A husband-and-wife team of historians explores the role of women and the struggle for women's rights; informative and interestingly written.

Page Smith, *America Enters the World*. New York: McGraw-Hill, 1985. This massive volume (over a thousand pages) details the period of the Progressive Era and World War I, with an emphasis on how events affected ordinary people. It is part of a multi-volume series, "People's History" by a leading expert on American history.

Edward B. Weinstock, *The Wilderness War*. New York: Julian Messner, 1982. A book detailing the history of the fight to preserve wilderness in America, by an essayist who specializes in nature writing.

William Whyte, ed., *Our American Land*. Washington, DC: U.S. Government Printing Office, 1987. A collection of short, informative, but dry essays by a variety of experts on issues regarding land use and conservation. Some address the Progressive era.

Charles F. Wilkinson, *The Eagle Bird: Mapping a New West*. New York: Vintage Books, 1993. These essays by an expert of western law contain small sections on the conservation efforts of the 1900s.

Index

Picture Credits

Cover photos: American Stock/Archive Photos (left) and Corbis-Bettmann (center and right)

American Stock/Archive Photos, 24, 43

Archive Photos, 8, 15, 53 (both), 60, 65, 69, 97, 106, 111

Archive Photos/Auburn Cord Duesenberg Museum, 74

Archive Photos/Camera Press, 59

Archive Photos/Museum of the City of New York, 10, 31, 37, 41

Corbis, 38

Corbis-Bettmann, 17, 20, 21, 30, 35, 56, 62, 72, 76, 80, 89, 102, 104, 110

© Henry Ford Museum, 85

Hirz/Archive Photos, 44

John Muir National Historic Site, 63

Library of Congress, 4, 6, 7, 11, 13, 26, 34, 47, 50, 52, 77, 87, 93, 101, 112, 113

Lineworks, Inc., 91, 92

Pach/Corbis-Bettmann, 109

Popperfoto/Archive Photos, 68

© Smithsonian Institution, 78

UPI/Corbis-Bettmann, 45, 55, 66

About the Author

Adam Woog, the author of a number of books for adults and young adults, lives in Seattle, Washington, with his wife and young daughter. His mother once slept under wool blankets taken by Robert Peary to the North Pole in 1909.

DATE DUE

MAY 0 8 2006			